The Best of *Bead&Button* Magazine

Beaded Necklaces

Compiled by Julia Gerlach and Tea Benduhn

Printed in the United States of America

06 07 08 09 10 11 12 13 14 10 9 8 7 6 5 4 3 2 1

ISBN-10: 0-87116-231-8
ISBN-13: 978-0-87116-231-1

Publisher's Cataloging-In-Publication Data
(Prepared by The Donohue Group, Inc.)

Beaded necklaces / compiled by Julia Gerlach and Tea Benduhn.

p. : ill. ; cm.

ISBN: 0-87116-231-8
Includes index.

1. Beadwork--Handbooks, manuals, etc. 2. Beadwork--Patterns. 3. Jewelry making--Handbooks, manuals, etc. 4. Necklaces. I. Gerlach, Julia. II. Benduhn, Tea. III. Title: Best of Bead&Button magazine IV. Title: Bead & Button.

TT860 .B43 2006
745.594/2

Managing art director: Lisa Bergman
Book layout: Sabine Beaupré
Photographers: Bill Zuback and Jim Forbes
Project editors: Tea Benduhn, Julia Gerlach, Cheryl Phelan

Acknowledgments: Mindy Brooks, Terri Field, Jim Forbes, Lora Groszkiewicz, Kellie Jaeger, Carrie Jebe, Diane Jolie, Patti Keipe, Alice Korach, Pat Lantier, Tonya Limberg, Debbie Nishihara, Carole Ross, Salena Safranski, Candice St. Jacques, Maureen Schimmel, Kristin Schneidler, Lisa Schroeder, Mike Soliday, Terri Torbeck, Helene Tsigistras, Annette Wall, Elizabeth Weber, Lesley Weiss, Bill Zuback

CONTENTS

INTRODUCTION

Necklaces are the perfect accessories. They can be created in nearly any style and are great for drawing attention to an outfit—and to the wearer. In *The Best of Bead&Button Magazine: Beaded Necklaces*, we've assembled more than 30 great necklace projects that use a variety of creative techniques.

For more than a decade, *Bead&Button* magazine has been a great resource for beaders looking for inspiration and expertise. Editor-tested step-by-step instructions and clear photos and illustrations make these projects easy to follow and complete. We've provided a reference section on the most common tools and materials as well as a helpful guide to the basic techniques of beading. Whether you are a novice beader or a more advanced devotee, you can assemble the perfect necklace to complete your look.

Beaded Necklaces features exciting pieces that employ a variety of techniques, including stringing, stitching, and wirework. Whether you go simple and streamlined or lacy and textured, you are sure to find several necklaces to suit your mood and wardrobe in this collection. Styles include lariats, chokers, Y-shaped, and more in a wide range of lengths and using a variety of materials. With so many different necklaces to chose from, you may have a hard time deciding which one to make first. Have a wonderful time—and let your creativity shine!

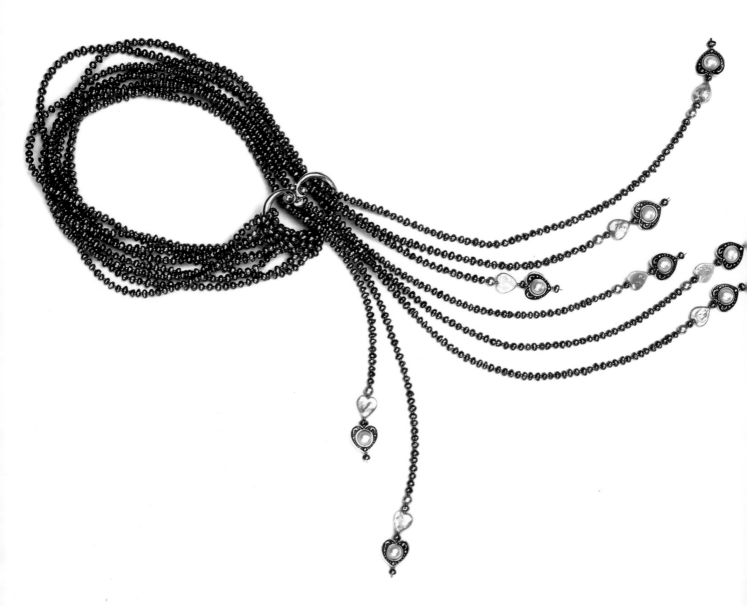

TOOLS AND MATERIALS

It's easy to make beautiful bead jewelry that's as good as or better than the jewelry you see in upscale department stores. If you can thread a cord or wire through a hole, you're more than halfway there. The big "secret" of the pros is knowing what tools and materials to use to get the best results. On the following pages you'll find descriptions of the most important tools you'll need, as well as commonly used findings and stringing materials.

FINDINGS

Findings are the parts that link beads into a piece of jewelry. Always buy the best metal findings you can afford. If you use inexpensive base metal, it may soon discolor. Pewter-based metal holds its finish well. Sterling silver and gold-filled findings usually increase the cost of a piece by less than $5 and look good for many years. Here are the key findings:

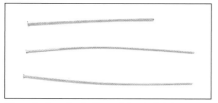

Head pins look like a blunt, thick sewing pins. They have a decorated or flat head on one end to hold the beads in place. Head pins come in different diameters, or gauges, and lengths ranging from 1–3 in. (2.5–7.6cm).

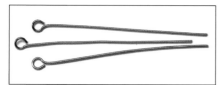

Eye pins are just like head pins except that they have a round loop on one end, instead of a head. You can make your own eye pins from wire.

Jump rings are a small wire circle or oval that is either soldered or comes with a split that you can twist open and closed.

Split rings are used like jump rings, but they are much more secure. They look like tiny key rings and are made of springy wire.

Crimp beads are small, large-holed, thin-walled metal beads designed to be flattened or crimped into a tight roll. Use them when stringing jewelry on flexible beading wire.

Clasps come in many sizes and shapes. Some of the most common are (from top to bottom) toggle, consisting of a ring and a bar; lobster claw, which opens when you push on a tiny lever; magnetic, which consists of two halves that attract each other; S-hook, which links two soldered rings or split rings; and hook and eye.

Cones usually are made of metal and look like pointed ice cream cones with openings at both ends. They are ideal for concealing the ends and knots of a multistrand necklace and joining it attractively to the clasp.

STRINGING MATERIALS

Flexible beading wire comes in several brands. They all consist of very fine wires that have been twisted or braided together and covered with a smooth plastic coating. Aculon, Beadalon, Soft Flex, and Accuflex are the most popular brands, and they all come in a variety of sizes. For many stringing projects, .014 and .015 work fine, but the weight of the finished piece determines what size you'll need. Use thicker varieties when using heavy beads or making pieces that receive a lot of stress. Thinner wire works well for lightweight pieces and beads with very small holes, such as pearls. Some wires are more flexible than others. The higher the number of inner strands (between seven and 49), the more flexible and kink-resistant the wire.

Bead cord is also commonly used for stringing beads. Made predominantly with braided synthetic fibers, some popular brands are Stringth and the thick upholstery thread Conso. They come in different thicknesses, which are indicated by numbers or letters; the higher the number or letter, the thicker the cord, except for O, which is usually the thinnest. No matter how thick or thin, bead cord can always be doubled when stringing.

Traditionally, pearls are strung on silk cord with a knot between each pearl, but many new nylon cords are almost as supple, much less stretchy than silk, and they knot beautifully.

Several different types of elastic cords are made expressly for beading. Some elastic cords have a round profile; others are opaque and fibrous. Both types come in a variety of colors.

Beading threads, primarily used for off-loom beadweaving, are often made with nylon; the most common is Nymo (the small spools shown above, left). Nymo comes in sizes O, B, and D, listed from thinnest to thickest size.

Recently, beaders have begun using fishing line in place of beading thread, specifically a brand called Fireline (above, right). Although it doesn't come in an assortment of colors, like Nymo does, its high-tech synthetic fibers make it a very resilient and strong thread. While it comes in various strengths, 6–10 lb. tests are most often used for beading projects.

Do not string beads on traditional monofilament fishing line, because it becomes brittle and snaps. Nor is sewing thread a good option for beadwork, as it is simply too weak.

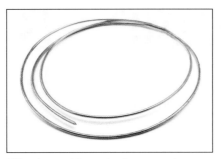

Wire is used to make loops and eye pins or to wrap beads creatively. The smaller the gauge, the thicker the wire. Memory wire is steel spring wire; it's used for coil bracelets, necklaces, and rings.

Do not use your jewelry-grade wire cutters on memory wire, which is extremely hard; use heavy-duty cutters, or bend it back and forth until it breaks.

TOOLS

You need very few tools for making bead jewelry, but don't use the large, grooved pliers in your family tool kit; they produce terrible results.

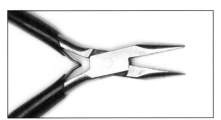

Chainnose pliers for jewelry making have smooth, flat inner jaws, and the tips taper to a point so you can get into tiny spaces. Use them for gripping and for opening and closing loops and rings. Some people call chainnose pliers **flatnose** because the inside of the jaw is flat. True flatnose pliers, however, do not come to a point at the tip, so they can't go everywhere that chainnose pliers can.

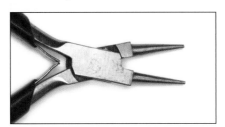

Roundnose pliers have smooth, tapered, conical jaws. You form loops around them. The closer to the tip of the pliers you make the loop, the smaller the loop will be.

On **diagonal wire cutters**, the outside (back) of the blades meets squarely, yielding a flat-cut surface. The inside of the blades makes a pointed cut. Always cut wire with the back of the blades against the section you want to use so the end will be flat.

Crimping pliers are used with tube-shaped crimp beads. Crimping pliers have two grooves in their jaws to enable you to fold or roll a crimp into a compact shape.

Split-ring pliers allow you to open split rings easily, without breaking your fingernails.

BASICS

To give your jewelry a professional touch and ensure that your treasures will stand up to frequent wearings, it's important to master a few basic techniques. Good knots, loops, and crimps make the difference between a piece you love to wear and one that sits in a drawer.

FUNDAMENTALS

conditioning thread
Use either beeswax (not candle wax or paraffin) or Thread Heaven to condition nylon thread (Nymo). Stretch the thread, then pull it through the conditioner, starting with the end that came off the spool first.

ending/adding thread
To end a thread, weave back into the beadwork, tying two or three half-hitch knots between beads as you go. Change directions as you weave so the thread crosses itself. Sew through a few beads after the last knot before cutting the thread. To add a thread, start several rows below the point where the last bead was added and weave through the beadwork, tying half-hitch knots between beads.

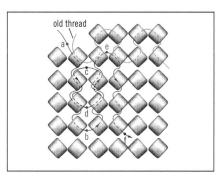

stop bead
Use a stop bead to secure beads temporarily when you begin stitching. Choose a bead that is different from the beads in your project. String the stop bead about 6 in. (15cm) from the end of your thread, and go back through it in the same direction. If desired, go through it one more time for added security.

KNOTS
Working with beading cords and threads like Nymo, Silamide, or Fireline often requires knots for security.

half-hitch knot
Exit a bead and form a loop perpendicular to the thread between beads. Bring the needle under that thread and away from the loop. Then go back over the thread and through the loop. Pull gently so the knot doesn't tighten prematurely.

lark's head knot
Fold a cord in half, and lay it behind a ring, loop, bar, etc. with the fold pointing down. Bring the ends through the ring from back to front, then through the fold, and tighten.

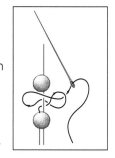

overhand knot
Cross the ends to make a loop. Bring the end that crosses in front behind the loop, and pull it through the loop to the front. Tighten.

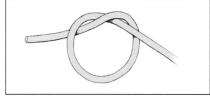

square knot
Bring the left-hand thread over the right-hand thread and around. Cross right over left, and go through the loop.

Twisted wire needles are made from a length of fine wire folded in half and twisted tightly together. They have a large, open eye at the fold, which is easy to thread. The eye flattens when you pull the needle through the first bead.

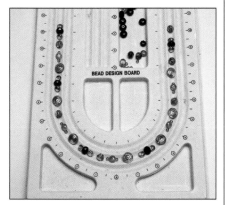

Beading needles look like long, extra thin sewing needles. The most frequently used sizes are #10 to 13. Higher numbers indicate a thinner needle.

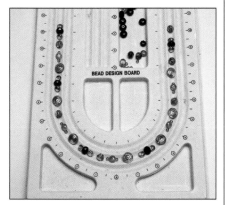

Bead design boards are an important tool for visualizing your design before you start stringing.

surgeon's knot

Bring the left-hand thread over the right-hand thread twice. Pull the ends to tighten. Cross right over left, and go through the Loop. Tighten.

pearl knotting

String a knotted necklace on doubled cord, starting with cord four times the desired finished length plus 8 in. (20cm). String a bead tip (if using them), all the beads, and the second bead tip. Push everything that will follow the first knot to the needle end of the cord.

1 Loop the cord around the first three or four fingers of your left hand (right for lefties) with the bead tip end on top.

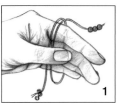

2 Pinch the cross between your thumb and index finger. Hold the cord circle open on your spread fingers with your palm up. Then drop the bead end of the cord through the circle into your hand.

3 Put a long T-pin or an awl into the loop the same way the cord goes through. Gradually tighten the loop as it slips off your fingers, keeping the awl in it. Slide the awl toward the spot

where you want the knot to be as you pull the bead end of the cord in the opposite direction. When the knot is right against the bead tip, let the cord slip off the tip of the awl. To set the knot, pull the two cord strands in opposite directions. Slide the next bead to the knot and repeat.

CRIMPING

Crimping, usually used to secure flexible beading wire to a clasp, is the process of flattening or folding a crimp bead securely on your stringing material. Flattened crimps require only a pair of chainnose pliers, while folded crimps require a pair of crimping pliers.

It's a good idea to place a bead between the crimp and the clasp to ease strain on the wire.

flattened crimp

1 Hold the crimp bead using the tip of your chainnose pliers. Squeeze the pliers to flatten the crimp.

2 Tug the clasp to make sure the crimp has a solid grip on the wire. If the wire slides, remove the crimp bead and repeat the steps with a new crimp bead.

folded crimp

1 Position the crimp bead in the notch closest to the crimping pliers' handle.

2 Separate the wires and firmly squeeze the crimp.

3 Move the crimp into the notch at the pliers' tip and hold the crimp as shown. Squeeze the crimp bead, folding it in half at the indentation.

4 Test that the folded crimp is secure.

WIRE LOOPS AND JUMP RINGS

Wire loops and jump rings are necessary any time you need to connect wire elements together, such as when attaching a beaded head pin to an earring wire.

If you've never worked with wire before, get some inexpensive craft or copper wire for your first attempts at making loops. Don't worry if your first loops aren't great; practice makes perfect. Your loops will be small if you form them closer to the tips of the pliers and larger if you hold the wire where the jaws are thicker.

jump rings: opening and closing

1 Hold a jump ring with two pairs of chainnose pliers or with chainnose and roundnose pliers.

2 To open the jump ring, bring the tips of one pair of pliers toward you and push the tips of the

other pair away. Reverse the steps to close the ring.

loops, plain

1 Trim the wire ⅜ in. (1cm) above the bead. Make a right-angle bend close to the bead.

2 Grab the wire's tip with roundnose pliers. Roll the wire to form a half circle. Release the wire.

3 Reposition the pliers in the loop and continue rolling.

4 The finished loop should form a circle centered above the bead.

loops, wrapped

1 Make sure you have no less than 1¼ in. (3.2cm) of wire above your bead. With the tip of your chainnose pliers, grasp the wire directly above the bead. Bend the wire above the pliers at a right angle.

2 Using roundnose pliers, position the jaws in the bend.

3 Bring the wire over the top jaw of the roundnose pliers.

4 Reposition the pliers so the lower jaw fits snugly in the loop. Curve the wire downward around the bottom of the roundnose pliers. This is the first half of a wrapped loop.

5 Position the jaws of your chainnose pliers across the loop.

6 Wrap the wire around the wire stem, covering the space between the loop and the bead. Trim the excess wire and gently press the cut end close to the wraps with chainnose pliers.

WIRE BASICS

Wire comes in thicknesses called gauges. The higher the gauge, the thinner the wire, so 20-gauge wire is thinner than 18-gauge. If the wire is too soft, it may not hold its shape, but if it's too hard, it will tend to break. Wire sold as "half-hard" is a good bet. Wire that's too hard can be softened by heating it with a torch. If your wire is too soft, you can harden it by hammering. Use a regular hammer with a smooth metal head if you also want to flatten the wire. If you want the wire to remain round, use a rawhide mallet. But beware: wire that has been hardened too much or twisted too many times breaks easily. It's best to harden it after bending. Don't hammer loops, because you might create a rough edge. To avoid marking your wire, wrap the jaws of your pliers with cloth tape. Always practice safety precautions when working with wire:

- Wear eye protection (safety glasses or the equivalent).
- When cutting wire, always hold both parts or cover them with your hand.
- File all exposed, cut ends smooth to prevent scratches or snags.

– Carol H. Straus

MAKING HEAD PINS

Make a tiny U-shaped loop at the end of the wire with the tip of a roundnose pliers, pinch it closed with chainnose pliers, and trim the wire end just after the bend.

BEAD EMBROIDERY

To stitch a line of beads, come up through the fabric from the wrong side. String three beads. Stretch the bead thread along the line where the beads will go, and go through the fabric right after the third bead. Come up through the fabric between the second and third beads and go through the third bead again. String three more beads and repeat. For a tighter stitch, string only two beads at a time.

FLAT, EVEN-COUNT PEYOTE

1 Pick up one bead and loop through it again in the same direction. Pick up beads to total an even number. These beads comprise the first two rows. (Remove the extra loop and weave the tail into the work after a few rows.)

2 Every other bead from step 1 drops down half a space to form row 1. To begin row 3 (count diagonally), pick up a bead and go through the second bead from the end. Pick up a bead and go through the fourth bead from the end. Continue in this manner. End by going through the first bead strung.

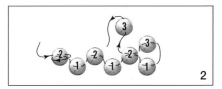

3 To start row 4 and all other rows, pick up a bead and sew through the last bead added on the previous row. Weave through the work in a zigzag path to end thread. Begin a thread the same way, exiting the last bead added in the same direction to resume.

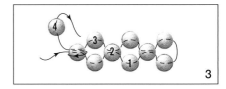

FLAT, ODD-COUNT PEYOTE

Begin as for flat, even-count peyote, but pick up an odd number of beads. Work row 3 as in even-count. Since the first two rows total an odd number of beads, you won't have a place to attach the last bead on odd-numbered rows.

1 Work a figure-8 turn at the end of row 3, which will position you to start row 4: String the next-to-last bead (#7) and go through #2, then #1. String the last bead (#8) and go through #2, #3, #7, #2, #1, and #8. You can continue to work this turn at the end of each odd-numbered row, but this edge will be stiffer than the other.

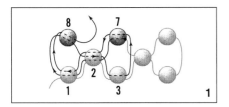

2 For a modified turn, string the last bead of the row then loop through the edge thread immediately below. Go through the last bead to begin the new row. Then turn at the end of even-numbered rows as shown.

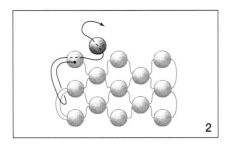

ZIPPING UP OR JOINING FLAT PEYOTE

To join two sections of peyote stitch invisibly, begin with a high bead on one side and a low bead on the other. Go through each high bead, alternating sides.

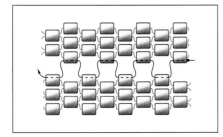

PEYOTE GRADUAL INCREASE

1 The gradual increase takes four rows. At the point of the increase, pick up two thinner beads. Go through the next up-bead.

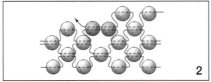

2 On the next row, when you get to the two thin beads, stitch through them as if they were one bead.

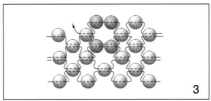

3 On the third row, place two regular-sized beads over the two thin beads.

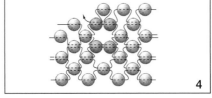

4 When you get to the two beads on the next row, go through the first, pick up a bead, and go through the second bead.

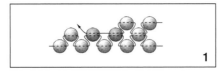

PEYOTE GRADUAL DECREASE

1 At the point of the decrease, go through two up-beads.

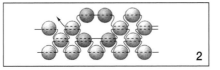

2 On the second row of the decrease, put two thin beads in the open space, and go through the next up-bead.

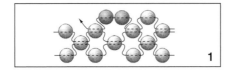

3 On the third row, go through the two thin beads as if they were one bead.

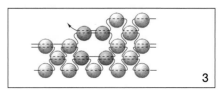

4 On the fourth row, pick up one bead, and go through the next up-bead.

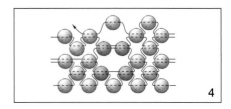

PEYOTE RAPID INCREASE

1 At the point of the increase, pick up two beads instead of one. Go through the next bead.

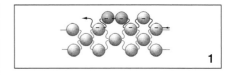

2 When you reach the two beads on the next row, go through the first bead, add a bead, and go through the second bead.

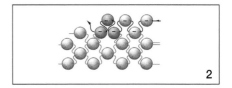

PEYOTE RAPID DECREASE

1 At the point of the decrease, go through two beads on the previous row.

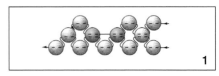

2 On the next row, when you reach the two-bead space, pick up one bead.

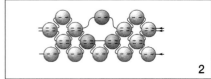

TWO-DROP PEYOTE

Work two-drop peyote stitch the same as basic peyote, but treat pairs of beads as if they were single beads. Start with an even number of beads divisible by four. Pick up two beads (stitch 1 of row 3), skip two beads, and go through the next two beads.

TUBULAR OR CIRCULAR EVEN-COUNT PEYOTE

1 Pick up beads to fit the desired circumference. You must use an even number of beads. Knot the thread to form a ring, leaving some slack.

2 Put the ring over a form if desired. Go through the first bead to the left of the knot. Pick up a bead, skip a bead on the previous round, and go through the next bead. Repeat around until you're back at the start.

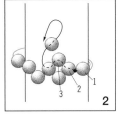

3 Since you started with an even number of beads, you need to step up to be in position to start the next round (round numbers are indicated in figures). Go through the first beads on rounds 2 and 3. Pick up a bead, and go through the second bead on round 3; continue.

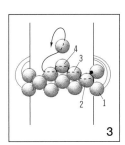

LADDER

1 A ladder of seed beads or bugle beads is used to begin brick stitch or herringbone. To make a ladder, pick up two beads, leaving a 6-in. (15cm) tail. Go through both beads again in the same direction. Pull the top bead down so the beads are side by side. The thread exits the bottom of the second bead (**a–b**). Pick up a third bead, and go back through the second bead from top to bottom.

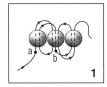

2 Come back up the third bead (**b–c**). String a fourth bead. Go through the third bead from bottom to top and the fourth bead from top to bottom (**c–d**). Continue adding beads until you reach the desired length.

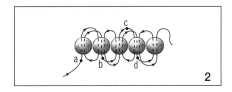

3 To reinforce the ladder, zigzag back through it.

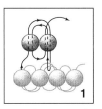

BRICK STITCH

1 Whenever possible, begin each brick stitch row so no thread shows on the edge. Pick up two beads. Go under the thread bridge between the second and third beads on the ladder from back to front. Go up the second bead added and then down the first. Come back up the second bead.

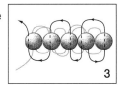

2 For the row's remaining stitches, pick up one bead. Go under the next thread bridge on the previous row from back to front. Go back up the new bead. Brick stitch naturally decreases by one bead at the start of each row.

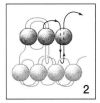

SQUARE STITCH

1 Pick up the required number of beads for the first row. Then pick up the first bead of the second row. Go through the last bead of the first row and the first bead of the second row in the same direction as before. The new bead sits on top of the old bead, and the holes are horizontal.

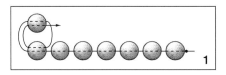

2 Pick up the second bead of row 2, and go through the next-to-last bead of row 1. Continue through the new bead of row 2. Repeat this step for the entire row.

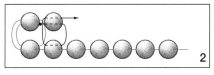

RIGHT-ANGLE WEAVE

1 To start the first row, string four beads and tie them into a ring. Go through the first three beads again.

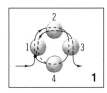

2 Pick up three beads (#5, #6, and #7). Go back through the last bead of the previous ring and continue through #5 and #6.

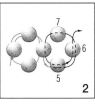

3 Pick up three beads, and go back through #6 and the first two new beads. Continue adding three beads for each stitch until the first row is the desired length. You are sewing rings in a figure 8 pattern, alternating direction with each stitch.

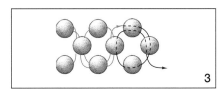

4 To begin row 2, go through the last three beads of the last stitch on row 1, exiting the bead at the edge of one long side.

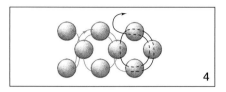

5 Pick up three beads, and go back through the bead you exited in the previous step. Continue through the first new bead.

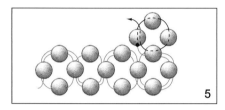

6 Pick up two beads, and go through the top bead on the previous row and the bead you exited on the previous stitch. Continue through the two new beads and the next top bead of the previous row.

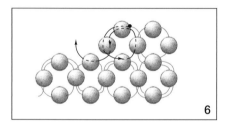

7 Pick up two beads, then go through the bead you exited on the previous stitch, the top bead on the previous row, and the first new bead. Keep the thread moving in a figure 8. Pick up two beads per stitch for the rest of the row. When you go back through, don't sew straight lines across stitches.

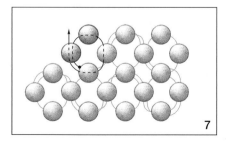

TUBULAR RIGHT-ANGLE WEAVE

When you are one stitch short of the desired circumference of the tube, connect the last stitch to the first stitch as follows: Exit the end bead of the last stitch, pick up one bead, go through the first bead of the first stitch, and pick up one bead. Complete the connecting stitch by retracing the thread path. Exit as shown above. In subsequent rows, you'll need to add only one bead to connect the ends.

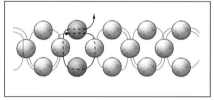

STRINGING

Four in one

Create cluster beads with a multi-strand technique

by **Terri Torbeck**

When it comes to beading, the struggle between *want* versus *need* can be daunting. If you find that you've acquired the perfect bead but aren't quite sure what do with it, here's a simple, elegant solution for highlighting the most artistic of beads.

Create the foundation
[1] Cut four strands of flexible beading wire 24 in. (61cm) long.
[2] Using all four strands as one piece, slide a crimp bead to the center of the wires. Crimp the bead (Basics, p. 7).
[3] Slide the focal bead over all the strands and center it over the crimp.

Use a pen to mark the wires at each edge of the focal bead. Slide the focal bead off.
[4] String a crimp bead on each end, over all four strands. Position each crimp ⅛ in. (3mm) inside the marks and crimp the crimp beads.
[5] Center the focal bead on the strands.

Make a beaded cluster
[1] Slide a 3mm flat spacer over all four strands and against the focal bead.
[2] Follow the stringing pattern for the four strands, alternating amber pebbles and flat spacers on two strands, and 2mm spacers and Czech glass beads on the other two strands (**figure**).

MATERIALS

necklace 17½ in. (45cm)

- large-hole artist bead (Ghost Cow Glassworks, ghostcow.com, 520-622-7199)
- **4** 15 x 18mm amber beads, disk shape
- 16-in. (41cm) strand 7–9mm amber pebbles
- 16-in. (41cm) strand 4mm Czech glass bicone beads
- **8** 17 x 15mm pierced Indian beads, sterling silver
- **4** 8 x 10mm flat sterling silver beads
- **36** 2mm beads, sterling silver
- **38** 3mm flat spacer beads, sterling silver
- **2** 6 x 3mm spacer beads, sterling silver
- S-hook, sterling silver
- 2 cones, sterling silver
- **15** crimp beads
- 6 in. (15cm) 18-gauge wire, sterling silver
- 2 in. (5cm) chain with 4mm links, sterling silver
- 2-in. (5cm) head pin, sterling silver
- flexible beading wire, .012–.014

Tools: chainnose pliers, crimping pliers, roundnose pliers, wire cutters, pencil or pen

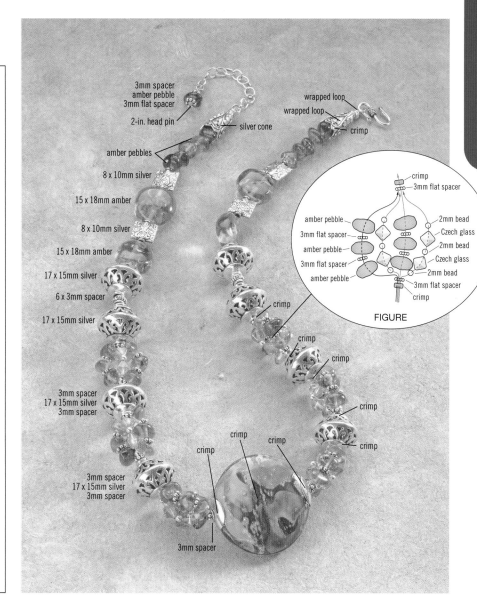

FIGURE

[3] Working one side of the necklace at a time, slide a flat spacer and a crimp over all the wires. Snug the spacer and crimp against the beaded strands. Pull each wire tight and crimp the crimp bead.
[4] String a silver accent bead over the crimp, and repeat steps 1 and 2 to string another bead cluster.
[5] Continue stringing accent beads and bead clusters until you have three clusters and three accent beads on each side of the necklace. String a 6 x 3mm spacer bead, an accent bead, a 15 x 18mm amber bead, an 8 x 10mm silver accent bead, a 15 x 18mm amber, an 8 x 10mm silver, and five amber pebbles over all four strands. Repeat on the other side (**figure**).

Finish the ends
[1] Slide a crimp bead over the four strands on one end of the necklace. Form a small loop by threading the ends of the wires back through the crimp bead. Snug the crimp against the last bead strung and crimp the crimp bead.
[2] Use a 3-in. (7.6cm) piece of 20-gauge wire and begin a wrapped loop near one end (Basics). Slide the crimped loop onto the wrapped loop. Finish the wrapped loop.
[3] Slide a cone on the wire and over the wrapped loop.
[4] Make a wrapped loop against the top of the cone. Trim excess wire.
[5] Repeat steps 1–3 on the other end of the necklace. Do not finish the wrapped loop above the cone.

Attach the closure
[1] Make the first half of a wrapped loop and slide the end link of a 2-in. (5cm) chain onto the loop. Finish the wrap and trim the excess wire.
[2] Thread a flat spacer, an amber pebble, and a flat spacer on a head pin. Begin a wrapped loop and connect it to the chain's end link. Finish the wrapped loop.
[3] Attach the S-hook to the wrapped loop on the other end.

Crystal clusters

Make every day a special occasion

*by **Anna Nehs***

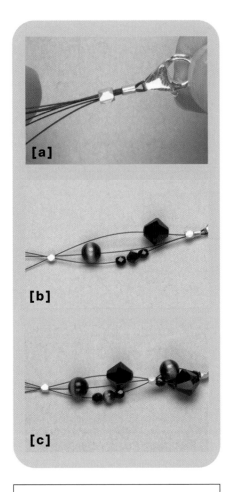

[a]

[b]

[c]

Crystals and sparkling, faceted beads are often reserved for special occasions. You don't have to wait for a holiday or fancy night out to drape yourself in twinkling shine, though. You can wear crystals any day, and feel like a princess.

[1] Cut three 26-in. (66cm) lengths of beading wire.

[2] Pass all three wires through a crimp bead, the loop on the clasp, and back through the crimp bead.

[3] Tighten the wire and crimp the crimp bead (Basics, p. 7).

[4] String a silver spacer over all the wires (**photo a**) and up to the crimp bead. Cut the three short wires as close to the silver spacer as possible.

[5] String an 8mm crystal on one wire and a 6mm bead on the second wire. String a 3mm crystal, a 4mm crystal, and a 3mm crystal on the remaining wire. Pass all three wires through a silver spacer (**photo b**).

[6] String an 8mm crystal on one wire and a 6mm bead on the second wire, as before. String a 3mm crystal, a 4mm round bead, and a 3mm crystal on the remaining wire. Pass all three wires through a silver spacer (**photo c**).

[7] Repeat steps 5 and 6 until you reach the desired length.

[8] Pass all three wires through a crimp bead and a soldered jump ring.

MATERIALS
necklace 17½ in. (45cm)

- **25–28** 8mm bicone crystals
- **13–16** 4mm bicone crystals
- **50–56** 3mm fire-polished glass beads
- **25–28** 6mm round glass beads
- **13–16** 4mm round glass beads
- **26–29** 3mm sterling silver spacers, square or round
- lobster claw clasp
- soldered jump ring
- 2 crimp beads
- flexible beading wire, .010, colored

Tools: crimping pliers, wire cutters

Bring the wire ends back through the crimp bead and the last silver spacer.

[9] Crimp the crimp bead and trim the excess wire.

Reinventing a pearl classic

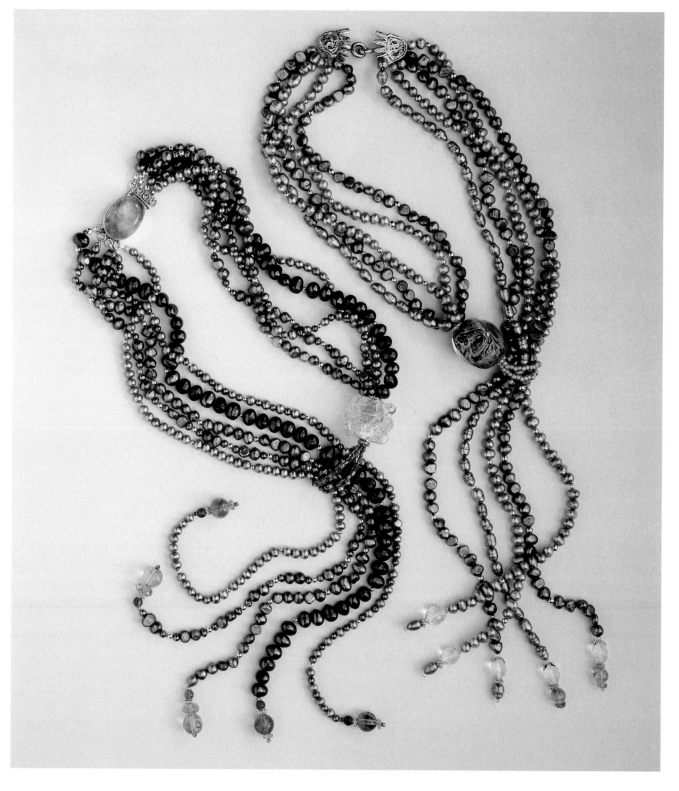

Create a lariat look with an art bead centerpiece

by **Alethia Donathan**

This faux lariat offers a fun update on the classic pearl necklace. With a bold art bead centerpiece and a variety of freshwater pearls, this necklace allows you to exhibit the luster and luxury of pearls, while including the sparkle and innovation of crystals and art glass. Using gold with silver emphasizes the natural variations in size, color, and shape found in freshwater pearls.

Tassel side

The tassel strands are 15 in. (38cm) long.

[1] Cut five 60-in. (1.5m) lengths of thread. Center an 11º seed bead on each strand. Bring both ends of each strand together and thread them both onto a twisted wire beading needle.

[2] Working with one needle at a time, string a pearl, a flat gold spacer, a faceted bead, and a seed bead (**photo a**). Repeat with two more strands.

[3] String the remaining two strands with an 8mm stone bead, a flat gold spacer, a faceted bead, and a seed bead.

[4] Continue stringing all five strands with pearls and round silver and gold beads. Make each strand different (**photo b**) and knot after every three to five pearls (Basics, p. 7) as you string.

[5] End each of two strands with an 11º seed bead. Knot after each 11º, then knot two strands together (**photo c**). String a bead tip over both needles, hinge side first, and tie the threads together inside the bead tip with one to three square knots (Basics). Seal this knot with glue.

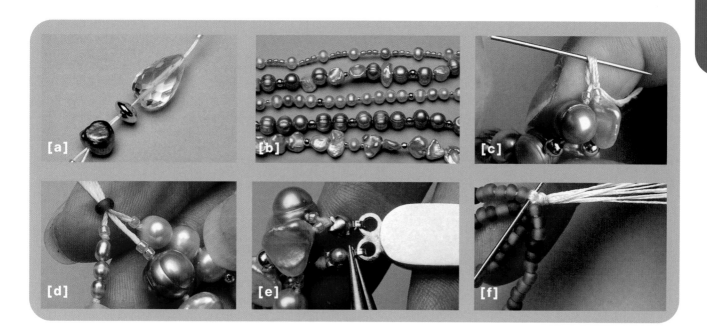

Once the glue is dry, trim the threads close to the knot and close the bead tip with chainnose pliers.

[6] For a two-strand clasp, end two of the remaining three strands with an 11º seed bead, as in step 5. End the last strand with two to three 11º seed beads. String an 8º seed bead over all three needles (**photo d**). Knot the strands together. String a bead tip over the threads, hinge end first, and end the threads as you did in step 5.

[7] Use roundnose pliers to attach each bead tip to the corresponding loop on a clasp half (**photo e**).

Focal bead side

[1] Cut five 40-in. (1m) lengths of thread.

[2] Thread a twisted wire beading needle onto two of the strands and string 2–3 in. (5–7cm) of 8º seed beads—enough to make a loop large enough to fit around the five strands of the tassel side and allow them to slide in and out of the loop. Make an identical loop by stringing seed beads on the remaining three strands. Center the bead loops on the strands and tie all ten threads together with an overhand knot

(Basics), sliding the knot snug against the loops (**photo f**).

[3] String a flat gold spacer, the focal bead, and a gold spacer over all ten threads.

[4] Separate the threads into pairs and thread a twisted wire beading needle on each pair. String five 8-in. (20cm) pearl strands to match the pearl strands on the other side of the necklace (**photo g**).

[g]

[5] End the strands as you did in steps 5–7 for the tassel side of the necklace. Thread the tassels through the loop to wear.

MATERIALS

necklace
- glass centerpiece bead with a medium-sized hole
- 5 6 x 9mm faceted stone or glass beads
- 2–3 16 in (41cm) strands each of 4 freshwater pearl shapes
- 2 8mm stone beads
- 50 3–4mm round gold beads
- 50 2–3mm round silver beads
- hank size 8º seed beads
- 2g size 11º seed beads
- 7 6mm flat spacers, gold
- 2- or 4-strand clasp, gold or silver
- 4–8 bead tips, gold or silver
- spool silk thread, size #2 (D)
- twisted wire beading needle
- G-S Hypo Cement

Tools: chainnose pliers, roundnose pliers, awl, pearl reamer

Wind swept necklace

String pearls and crystals through an elegant art bead

by **Alice Korach**

Carol Fonda and Monty Clark make a variety of delicately colored, free-form art glass beads. The bead used here is called "Wind swept" and is reminiscent of a cresting wave. Carol's daughter, Michelle Fisch, created the green necklace with pearls, pressed glass, and 6º seed beads. The author's pink version on the far left adds a triple fringe that dangles from inside the art bead.

Green necklace

[1] Cut a 24-in. (61cm) length of flexible beading wire. Attach a hemostat or clip to one end to keep the beads from falling off the wire. String a crimp bead and a bead with a large enough hole to accommodate two passes. Then string a random pattern of beads, alternating pearls, pressed glass, and seed beads for half the length of the necklace minus the length of the art bead (about 8 in./ 20cm). String the art bead (**photo a**).
[2] String an assortment of beads to fit inside the art bead. The last of these beads needs to be large enough to anchor the beads inside the art bead (**photo b**).

[a]

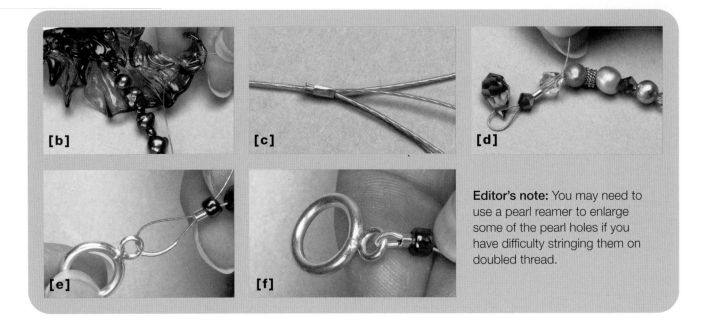

[b]

[c]

[d]

[e]

[f]

Editor's note: You may need to use a pearl reamer to enlarge some of the pearl holes if you have difficulty stringing them on doubled thread.

[3] String another bead to anchor the second half of the strand outside the art bead, and then string a random pattern of pearls, pressed glass, and seed beads to create the second half of the necklace. String a bead with a hole large enough to accommodate a second pass of wire and a crimp bead, then use a hemostat or clip to hold the beads in place.

Purple necklace

[1] Cut one 24-in. (61cm) and three 8-in. (20cm) lengths of flexible beading wire. Center a crimp on the 24-in. strand. Slide one end of each 8-in. wire into the crimp bead and crimp the crimp bead (Basics, p. 7 and **photo c**).

[2] Working on the side of the crimp bead with a single strand, string a large-holed bead over the crimp.

[3] String beads to fit inside the length of the art bead. End with a bead large enough to fit snugly inside the narrow end of the art bead. String the art bead, larger opening first, over the beads. Adjust the beads that fill the art bead as needed.

[4] String a repeating or random pattern on both ends of the 24-in. wire until you reach the desired length of the necklace, minus the length of the clasp. Then string a crimp bead on each end and secure the beads on the strands with hemostats or clips.

[5] String an assortment of beads on one of the 8-in. wires. End the dangle with a bead you can go through twice, a crimp bead, another bead you can go back through, and a drop bead. Skip the drop and go back through the last three beads (**photo d**). Leave a little slack so the dangle hangs nicely; you don't want it to be stiff. Crimp the crimp bead (Basics) and trim the excess wire.

[6] Repeat step 5 with the remaining 8-in. strands, making each one a different length.

Finishing

[1] Cut a ⅜ in. (1cm) piece of bullion wire with sharp scissors. Remove the hemostat or clip at one end of the necklace. Carefully thread on the bullion wire and a clasp half. Do not pinch or stretch the bullion wire. Bring the flexible beading wire back through the crimp bead and the last bead strung (**photo e**).

[2] Slowly tighten the beading wire so the bullion wire forms a neat loop that holds the clasp. Tighten the wire, but don't buckle the bullion (**photo f**). If the bullion wire becomes distorted, try again with a new piece. If the loop isn't tight enough, the wire will spread and won't protect the stringing material. Once the wire is tight, crimp the crimp bead (Basics) and trim the excess wire.

[3] Remove excess slack in the necklace and repeat steps 1 and 2 on the other end of the necklace.

MATERIALS

necklace

- "Wind swept" glass bead by Carol Fonda and Monty Clark (530-878-7483; dichroic-glass.com)
- **115–200** assorted pearls, crystals, Czech glass beads, size 6º seed beads, and silver spacers
- **3** top-drilled drop beads for dangle version (optional)
- toggle clasp
- crimp beads
- bullion wire, fine gauge
- flexible beading wire, .014

Tools: 2 hemostats or alligator clips, crimping pliers, wire cutters

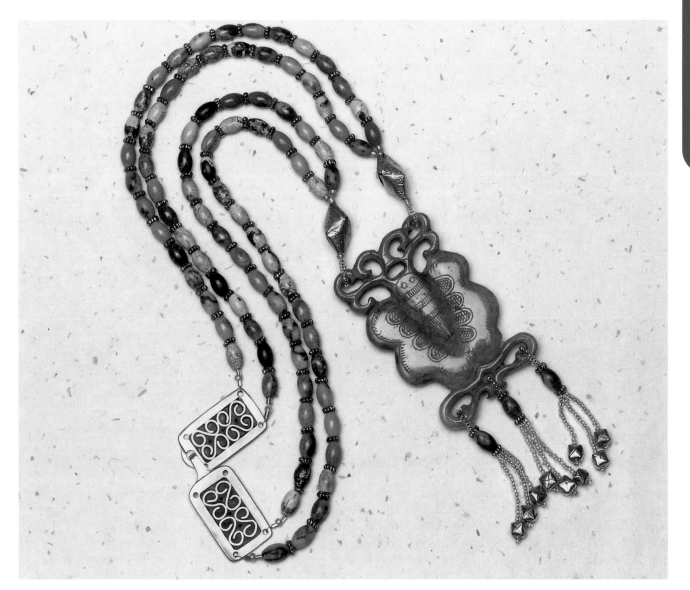

Fringed pendant

Connect strands to a pendant for a necklace that offers plenty of possibilities

by **Pam O'Connor**

This carved stone pendant is one-of-a-kind, but pendants are so popular it's easy to find them in bead stores and catalogs. For this necklace, pick one that has several openings for attaching the necklace strands and fringe.

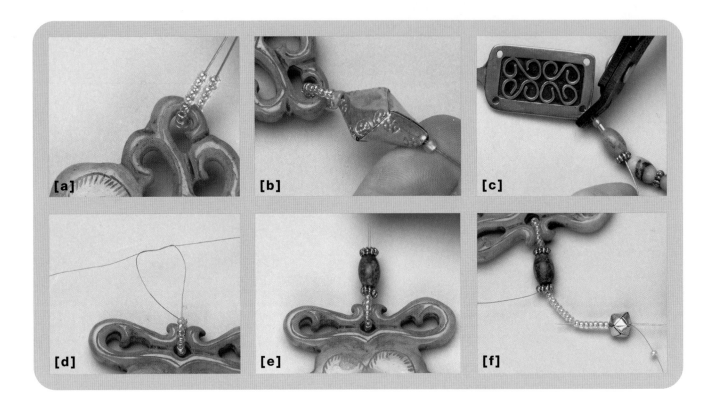

Make the necklace

[1] Cut a 26-in. (66cm) length of flexible beading wire. String enough 11º seed beads to make a small loop that will encircle the pendant opening where you will attach one side of the necklace. Center the seed beads on the wire.

[2] Slide an end of the wire through the pendant opening. Center the pendant over the seed beads, curving the wire in half (**photo a**).

[3] Slide an 8º seed bead, a 20 x 10mm bead, and an 8º over both ends of the wire (**photo b**).

[4] String an 8º on one wire end. Then string an alternating pattern of oblong stone beads and spacer beads for 10 in. (25cm).

[5] String a crimp bead, an 8º, and a crimp bead on the strand. Pass the wire through a clasp loop or hole. Go back through the 8º, the crimp beads, and a few more beads on the strand. Tighten the loop and crimp the crimp beads (Basics, p. 7 and **photo c**).

[6] Repeat steps 4 and 5 with the other wire end, attaching it to the second loop or hole on the same half of the clasp.

[7] Repeat steps 1–6 to string the necklace's other side.

String the fringe

[1] Thread a needle with 1 yd. (.9m) of Fireline. String enough 11º seed beads to make a small loop that will encircle the pendant opening where you will attach fringe. Leave a 6-in. (15cm) tail and pass the needle through the pendant opening. Tie the working thread and tail together in a surgeon's knot (Basics and **photo d**).

[2] String a spacer bead, an oblong bead, and a spacer bead over the working thread and tail (**photo e**). String 15–20 seed beads, a 7mm bead, and a seed bead.

[3] Skip the last seed bead, and sew back through the fringe beads (**photo f**). Continue sewing through the oblong bead, the spacer beads, and the bead loop. Sew through the spacer beads and oblong beads again, exiting the bottom spacer bead.

[4] String 15–20 seed beads, a 7mm bead, and a seed bead. Repeat step 3.

[5] Repeat step 4. To finish the thread, tie several half-hitch knots

(Basics) between beads, sew through a few beads, and trim.

[6] Repeat steps 1–5 to make fringe at other openings on the pendant.

MATERIALS

necklace 25 in. (34cm)
- 20–30mm carved pendant (Beauty & the Beads, 941-952-0101)
- 3 16-in. strands (41cm) 10 x 5mm oval stone beads
- 2 20 x 10mm gold-filled beads
- 9 7mm gold-filled beads
- 16-in. strand brass spacer beads
- 12 size 8º seed beads
- 5g size 11º seed beads
- 2-strand clasp
- 4 crimp beads
- Fireline, 6 lb. test
- flexible beading wire, .012–.014
- beading needles, #12

For a few links more

by **Irina Miech**

Turn leftover chain and head pins
into a lavish tassel for an art bead

Glass beadmaker Ron Galbraith makes
an outstanding selection of long, hollow
borosilicate (Pyrex) glass beads that
are perfect for the focal point of
a necklace. You can unify the art
bead with a simple
strand of elegant glass
beads and faceted stones
by hanging a complementary
tassel below the bead.

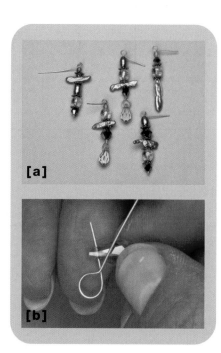

Make the tassel

[1] To make the dangles for the tassel, string head pins with small pearls, crystals, and silver spacers, ranging in length from 1–1½ in. (2.5–3.8cm). Begin a wrapped loop above the beads on each dangle (Basics, p. 7 and **photo a**).

[2] For the crystal drops, use a 3-in. (7.6cm) piece of 24-gauge wire and make the first half of a wrapped loop at one end. Slide the drop onto the loop (**photo b**) and finish the wrap. Now string an assortment of beads on the wire as in step 1 and start a second wrapped loop. You should make 21 dangles total.

[3] To assemble the tassel, cut a five-link piece of chain, approximately 1 in. (2.5cm) long. String a long dangle on the bottom link and complete the wraps. String a dangle on each side of the second link so that the bottom link separates them. String two dangles on each side of the third (**photo c**), fourth, and fifth links.

[a]

[b]

[4] Start a wrapped loop near one end of a 6 in. (15cm) piece of 20-gauge wire. Connect the loop to the fifth link (**photo d**). Make one or two wraps and trim the short wire.

[5] Connect two dangles on each side of the loop. Then string a 6mm crystal and a spacer on the wire. String the art bead (**photo e**), a spacer, and a 6mm crystal. Make a wrapped loop above the beads just strung.

String the necklace

[1] Arrange the larger beads and silver spacers for the necklace on a design board. Create your own pattern, or refer to the necklace above or on p. 25.

[2] Center the loop above the art bead on a 22 in. (56cm) length of beading wire. Then string the sides of the necklace as arranged on the design board, ending with a crimp bead on each end (**photo f**).

[3] Cut the 8–10 in. (20–25cm) piece of chain into two equal lengths.

[4] Working on one end of the necklace at a time, bring the end of the flexible beading wire through the end link of one of the chain pieces and back through the crimp.

MATERIALS

both projects

- 45 x 20mm lampwork bead
- **38** 8mm flat silver spacers
- **2** 6mm bicone crystals
- **100–125** 4–6mm assorted pearls, crystals, and Czech glass beads
- **50-60** 4mm flat silver spacers
- S-hook clasp
- 6 in. (15cm) 20-gauge wire, half-hard
- 6 in. (15cm) 24-gauge wire, half-hard (optional)
- 8–10 in. (20–25cm) chain with links large enough to accommodate the S-hook clasp
- 1 in. (2.5cm) or five links of large, flat drawn cable chain
- **21** 2 in. (5cm) head pins
- **2** crimp beads
- flexible beading wire, .014–.019

glass bead necklace (p. 25)
16–24 in. (40.6–61cm)

- **10** 9 x 15mm glass beads
- **10** 10 x 14mm faceted smoky quartz beads
- **22** 6–7mm faceted pearls
- **9** stick pearls with a vertical hole

amber necklace (p. 26)
16–24 in. (40.6–61cm)

- **10** 12 x 18mm amber beads
- **10** 14 x 10mm faceted aquamarine beads
- **22** 6mm bicone crystals, jet 2x AB
- **9–12** 4 x 11mm drop crystals

Tools: chainnose pliers, crimping pliers, roundnose pliers, wire cutters, design board

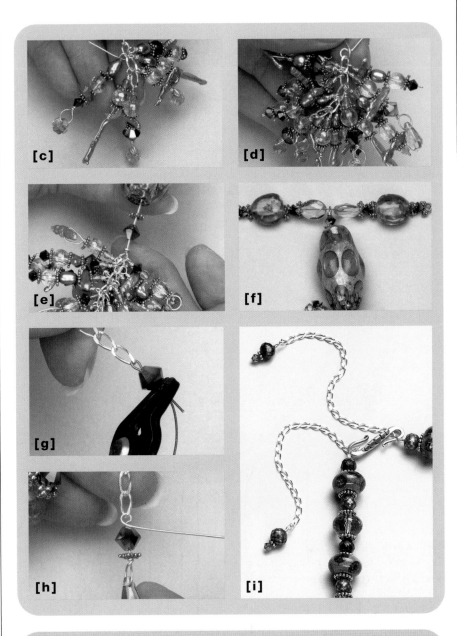

[c]

[d]

[e]

[f]

[g]

[h]

[i]

Crimp the crimp bead (Basics and **photo g**).

[5] Repeat at the other end. Make a short dangle on each of the two remaining head pins by stringing a bead or two and starting a wrapped loop. Connect one dangle to the end of each chain and complete the wraps (**photo h**). Connect one end of the S-hook to a link on each chain (**photo i**).

Editor's note: Instead of buying head pins, you can bend the end of 24-gauge wire lengths to make your own (Basics).

You can hang stick pearls as you would crystals drops. Instead of making a loop, string the stick pearl a third of the way down the wire. Bring the wire up along the sides of the pearl and bend the longer end so it points straight up above the pearl. Wrap the short end around the long end, as in a wrapped loop. String two or three beads above the wraps and begin a second wrapped loop.

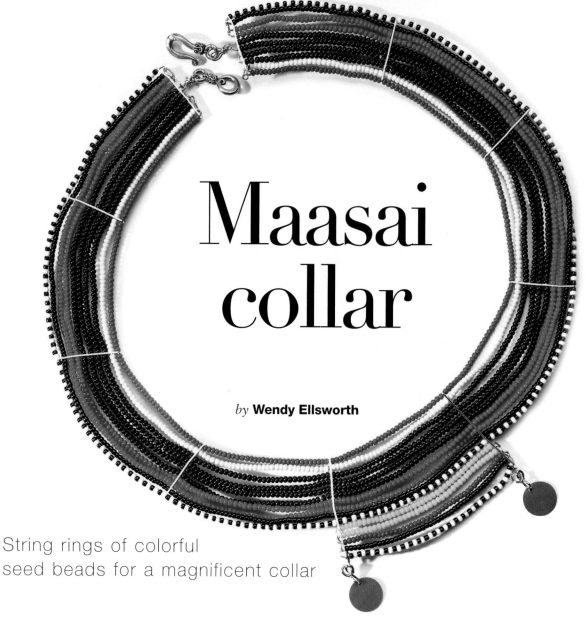

Maasai collar

by **Wendy Ellsworth**

String rings of colorful
seed beads for a magnificent collar

Kenya's Maasai people often wear colorful beaded collars made in a range of sizes, some large enough to fit over their heads and others with clasps. By necessity, they make their own separator bars. They use seed beads in opaque colors and often hang metal disks from the last row.

To keep the necklace flat, increase the number of beads per section by one or two beads with each new row. Bead sizes aren't uniform, however, so adjust the count as necessary.

[1] Cut the following six lengths of wire: 16 in. (41cm), 40 in. (1m), 44 in. (1.1m), 46 in. (1.2m), 50 in. (1.3m), and 54 in. (1.4m).

Row 1: a. Pass 2 in. (5cm) of the 40-in. wire through the first hole in a 10-hole separator bar. Bend the 2-in. wire tail to secure it.

b. Slide approximately 30 red beads onto the working end of the wire and string a separator bar through the first hole (**photo a**). Repeat twice (four separator bars in place). For the fifth and sixth bars, use the 15-hole separators (**photo b**).

c. Continue adding beads and separators until you have strung a total of 10 bars.

Row 2: a. Pass the working end of the wire back through the second hole of the end separator bar.

b. String enough white beads in each section so the bars lay flat when you shape the necklace into a circle. Go through the second hole on each bar (**photo c**).

c. When you go through the end bar, tighten the wire by pulling on it with pliers, then twist the wire ends together (**photo d**). Don't cut the wires yet.

Row 3: a. Pass the 44-in. wire through the third hole of the tenth bar (opposite the starting point) and bend a 2-in. tail to secure the wire.

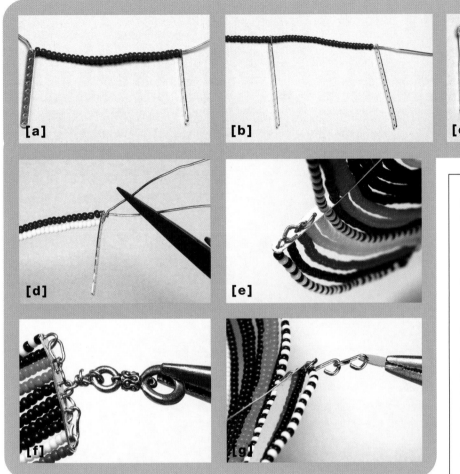

[a] [b] [c]

[d] [e]

[f] [g]

MATERIALS

- hank (or less) size 10º seed beads in each of the following colors: opaque red, white, black, blue, yellow, and orange
- **8** 10-hole sterling silver separator bars (Rio Grande, 800-545-6566, riogrande.com)
- **2** 15-hole sterling silver separator bars (Rio Grande)
- toggle clasp
- **2** small silver disks with chain or jump rings (optional)
- 25-ft. roll 22-gauge nickel silver wire (Hagstoz Jewelry Supply, 215-922-1627)

Tools: chainnose pliers, wire cutters

b. String blue beads, keeping the necklace flat, as before. Go through the third hole of each bar.

Row 4: a. Take the wire back through the fourth hole in the end bar.

b. String blue beads as in **Row 3**, using the fourth hole of each bar.

c. When the row is complete, tighten the wire and twist the ends together.

Rows 5 and **6:** Repeat **Rows 3** and **4** using the 46-in. wire and blue beads, starting at the first bar.

Rows 7 and **8:** Repeat **Rows 3** and **4** with the 50-in. wire and orange beads, starting at the tenth bar.

Rows 9 and **10:** Repeat **Rows 3** and **4** with the 54-in. wire, starting at the first bar. Use black beads for **Row 9** and alternate between black and white beads for **Row 10**.

Rows 11–15: a. Pass 2 in. of the 16-in. wire through the eleventh hole of one 15-hole separator bar, so the long section is between the bars. Secure the wire tail.

b. String enough yellow beads to span the space between the two bars. Go through the eleventh hole and back through the twelfth hole.

c. Work back and forth between the separator bars, changing colors as desired. Keep the wire tight and the tension firm.

d. When you're done stringing, weave the wire through the loops on the outside of the separator bars. Cut the wire and bend the tip around a loop (**photo e**).

[2] Use the wires from **Rows 5** and **6** to attach one end of the toggle clasp.

Cross the two wire ends through the clasp loop and wrap the ends as shown in **photo f**. Trim the wires and press the tips against the wraps.

[3] To attach the other end of the toggle, take one wire from **Rows 3** or **4** and one from **Rows 7** or **8** and weave them across the bar to the loop at **Rows 5** and **6** (the center of the bar). Then attach the clasp as in step 2.

[4] Weave the remaining wire tails through a loop or two, trim the ends, and bend the tips against loops.

[5] Add metal disks to the center separator bars with chain or jump rings, if desired (**photo g**).

Braided gemstone collar

by **Mindy Brooks**

Braid gemstone chips for a lush collar

This substantial gemstone necklace is easier to make than it looks. It only requires a few basic beading skills and the ability to make a simple braid.

Before you start, determine the finished length of your necklace, so you can make adjustments in advance. This one begins with a dozen 20-in. (51cm) beaded strands, which gives a 16-in. (41cm) braid. To make a longer necklace, add about 1¼ in. (3.2cm) of beads for every extra inch (2.5cm) of braid. Increase the length of the beading cord proportionately.

[1] Center a needle on a 60-in. (1.5m) length of Fireline or cord. String a seed bead and go through a bead tip the hook end first (**photo a**). Slide the seed bead and bead tip to about 5 in. (13cm) from the tail ends.
[2] Center a second needle on another 60-in. cord. Go through the same bead tip in the same direction as before, but without adding a seed

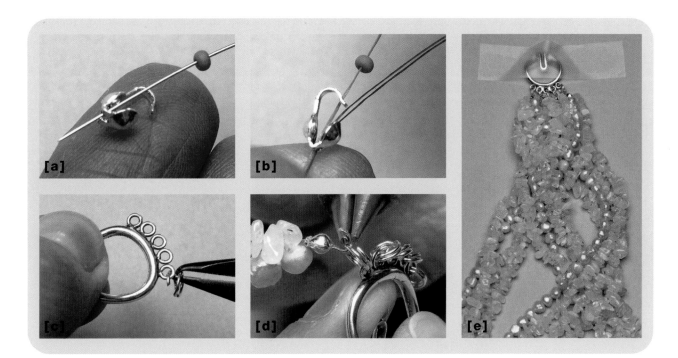

[a]   [b]   [c]   [d]   [e]

bead. You now have two pairs of tails coming out of the bead tip (**photo b**).

[3] Slide the seed bead into the bead tip and knot the tails together over the seed bead with several surgeon's knots (Basics, p. 7). Glue the knots and let them dry before trimming the excess cord. Using chainnose pliers, pinch the bead tip closed to hide the knots.

[4] String 20 in. (51cm) of chips or pearls on each strand. Cut off the needle at the fold and secure the ends with tape.

[5] To make the necklace shown at left, repeat steps 1–4 to string nine strands of gemstones and three of pearls. Vary the number of strands and bead combinations as desired.

[6] Open a split ring using your thumbnail or split-ring pliers. Attach one split ring to each loop on your clasp (**photo c**).

[7] Using roundnose pliers, roll each bead tip's hook around a split ring (**photo d**). Divide the bead tips as evenly as you can among the split rings, placing more strands on the middle rings, if necessary.

[8] Tape the clasp to your work surface to secure it. Divide the strands into three equal groups. To braid the necklace, cross an outer group over the center strands, then repeat with the group on the opposite side (**photo e**). Keep the tension even and relaxed.

[9] As you reach the end, you'll notice that the strands are now different lengths. Check the braid to make sure there are no gaps between beads, then string a few extra beads or take off a few where necessary so the strands are approximately even.

[10] Once the braid is finished, it isn't necessary to keep the strands in order. Choose two neighboring strands and string one bead tip onto the two pairs of tails. (This time go through the hinge end of the bead tip.) String a seed bead on one of the pairs. Knot the tails, glue the knots, trim the excess cord, and close the bead tips as in step 3. Repeat to finish the remaining pairs of strands.

[11] Attach split rings to the other clasp half as in step 6. Roll each bead tip's hook around a split ring as in step 7.

MATERIALS

necklace 17½ in. (45cm)

- **6** 36-in. (.9m) strands moonstone or other gemstone chips
- **4** 16-in. (41cm) strands freshwater pearls
- **12** size 11º seed beads
- multi-strand clasp (Ashes to Beauty Adornments, 505-899-8864)
- **12** bead tips
- **10** split rings
- Fireline, 6 lb. test or nylon beading cord, size 1 or 2
- extra-long beading needles, #12 or twisted wire needles
- G-S Hypo Cement

Tools: chainnose pliers, roundnose pliers, split-ring pliers (optional)

Dream weaving

Blend colors and textures for a ten-strand necklace

by **Karmen Schmidt**

Here's the perfect project to highlight your favorite focal bead. This necklace incorporates interwoven strands for a delicate, loose appearance. To accomplish the look, select your focal bead then choose complementary accent beads, carefully considering size, color, style, and texture. Plan your color scheme, using no more than three colors found in the focal bead. White, black, and metallic beads may be added, but should not be factored into the color count. As you systematically count beads and string strands, you shape a necklace sure to become a conversation starter. The instructions and diagrams may look advanced, but once you start beading, you'll find this as easy as counting to ten.

String the spine

[1] Cut the 18-gauge wire in half. Make a wrapped loop (Basics, p. 7) at one end. Repeat with the second wire.

[2] Cut a 4-yd. (3.7m) length of conditioned thread. Bring one end of the thread through a wire loop from step 1. Leaving a 3-in (7.6cm) tail, tie the thread to the loop with two square knots (Basics, p. 7).

[3] Now determine the length of one side of the spine by dividing the length of the necklace in half and subtracting 1 in. (2.5cm). (This one is 11 in./ 28cm.) String 6º seed beads, leaving a little slack between the end bead and the loop (**photo a**) until you reach the determined length. Make sure the seed count is divisible by ten. (This necklace uses 100 6º seed beads.)

[4] Attach the wire loop to a macramé board with T-pins. String the focal bead and the same number of 6ºs as on the other side.

[5] Go through the second wire loop. Tie two square knots, leaving slack between the end bead and the loop. Turn the board so the working thread is on your right, if you are right-handed, or your left, if you are left-handed.

[a]

Weave the strands

Refer to the illustrations on p. 34 as you weave the following ten strands. End and add thread (Basics) as needed, securing the tails only in the weaving strands. Don't knot the threads to the spine. Seal the knots with glue, if desired.

[1] **Strand one:** Go through the end bead on the spine. String enough 11º seed beads (one color) to span nine spine beads and go through the tenth spine bead (**photo b**). Repeat as shown, mixing 11ºs and accent beads. When you reach the center of the spine, sew through the focal bead. Work the second half in the mirror image of the first. Continue until you reach the other spine end bead.

[2] Go through the wire loop. Tie two square knots, leaving slack between the end bead and the loop. Turn the board and reverse the direction of the needle.

[3] **Strand two:** Go through the end bead. String enough 11ºs (one color) to span eight spine beads and go through the ninth spine bead (**photo c**). Now string enough 11ºs and accent beads to span nine spine beads as in step 1. Go through the tenth spine bead. Repeat until you reach the focal bead. Go through the focal bead and the next spine bead. Work the second half of the necklace as the mirror image of the first until there are nine spine beads before the wire loop. String enough 11ºs to span eight spine beads then go through the end bead. Repeat step 2.

[4] **Strand three:** Go through the end bead. String enough 11ºs to span seven spine beads and go through the eighth spine bead (**photo d**). String enough 11ºs and accent beads to span nine spine beads. Weave the strand around or between the two other strands then go through the tenth spine bead. Repeat until you've gone through the second spine bead from the focal bead. String enough seed beads to span one spine bead and go through the focal bead. Work the second half of the necklace as the mirror image of the first. Repeat step 2.

Stringing sequence

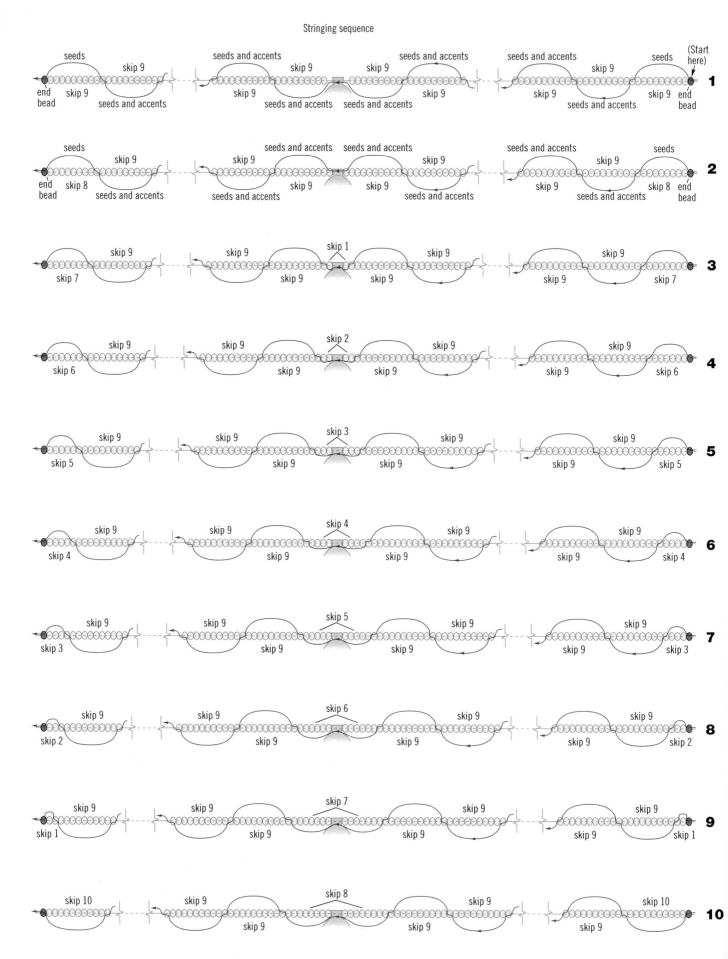

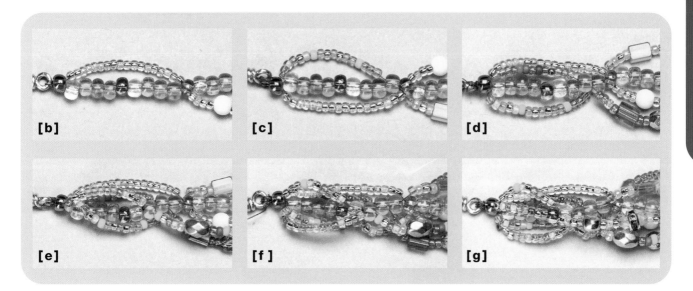

[b] [c] [d]

[e] [f] [g]

[5] Strand four: Go through the end bead. String enough 11°s (mixed colors) to span six spine beads and go through the seventh spine bead (**photo e**). String enough 11°s and accent beads to span nine spine beads. Weave around or between the strands then go through the tenth spine bead. Repeat until you've gone through the third spine bead from the focal bead. String enough seeds and accents to span two spine beads and go through the focal bead. Work the second half of the necklace as the mirror image of the first. Repeat step 2.

[6] Strand five: Go through the end bead. String enough 11°s to span five spine beads and go through the sixth spine bead (**photo f**). String enough 11°s and accents to span nine spine beads. Weave in the strand then go through the tenth spine bead. Repeat until you've gone through the fourth spine bead from the focal bead. String enough seeds and accents to span three spine beads and go through the focal bead. Work the second half of the necklace as the mirror image of the first. Repeat step 2.

[7] Strand six: Go through the end bead. String enough 11°s to span four spine beads and go through the fifth spine bead (**photo g**). String enough 11°s and accents to span nine spine beads. Weave in the strand then go through the tenth spine bead. Repeat until you've gone through the fifth spine bead from the focal bead. String enough seeds and accents to span four spine beads and go through the focal

bead. Work the second half of the necklace as the mirror image of the first. Repeat step 2.

[8] Strand seven: Go through the end bead. String enough 11°s to span three spine beads and go through the fourth spine bead. String enough 11°s and accents to span nine spine beads. Weave in the strand then go through the tenth spine bead. Repeat until

you've gone through the sixth spine bead from the focal bead. String enough seeds and accents to span five spine beads and go through the focal bead. Work the second half of the necklace as the mirror image of the first. Repeat step 2.

[9] Strand eight: Go through the end bead. String enough 11°s to span two spine beads and go through the third

spine bead. String enough 11ºs and accents to span nine spine beads. Weave in the strand then go through the tenth spine bead. Repeat until you've gone through the seventh spine bead from the focal bead. String enough seeds and accents to span six spine beads and go through the focal bead. Work the second half of the necklace as the mirror image of the first. Repeat step 2.

[10] Strand nine: Go through the end bead. String enough 11ºs to span one spine bead and go through the second spine bead. String enough 11ºs and accents to span nine spine beads. Weave in the strand then go through the tenth spine bead. Repeat until you've gone through the eighth spine bead from the focal bead. String enough seeds and accents to span seven spine beads and go through the focal bead. Work the second half of the necklace as the mirror image of the first. Repeat step 2.

[11] Strand ten: Go through the end bead. String enough 11ºs to span ten spine beads and go through the eleventh spine bead. String enough seeds and accents to span nine spine beads. Weave in the strand then go through the tenth spine bead. Repeat until you've gone through the ninth

spine bead from the focal bead. String enough seeds and accents to span the eight spine beads and go through the focal bead. Work the second half of the necklace as the mirror image of the first. Repeat step 2.

Attach the clasp

[1] String a cone, a spacer, and a 6mm accent bead onto the wire as shown below. Slide the cone over the loop and bead strands.

[2] Make the first half of a wrapped loop, slide the clasp onto the loop, and finish the wraps. Repeat on the other side.

MATERIALS
24-in. (61cm) necklace
- focal bead with large hole (dichroic pendant, above, from Eclectica, 262-641-0910)
- 16g size 6º seed beads,
- 96–160g size 11º seed beads in three colors
- **200–400** 2–6mm accent beads in three colors and various shapes
- **20–40** 2–3mm metal beads
- **2** 5–6mm accent beads
- **2** 5–6mm flat spacer
- **2** cones with ½-in. (13mm) diameter
- 8 in. (.2m) 18-gauge wire
- Fireline 6–8 lb. test or Nymo B conditioned with Thread Heaven
- beading needles, #12
- macramé board with T pins (optional)
- G-S Hypo Cement (optional)

Tools: chainnose pliers, roundnose pliers, wire cutters

STITCHING

Tiger gradation necklace

Learn great tricks for blending seed bead colors

by **Dina Krieg**

The inspiration for this necklace is a handmade glass tiger bead by Kathy Perras. It is set off in a simple design of complementary-colored seed beads that bring out its rich patterning.

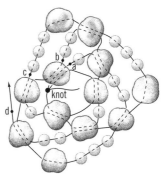

FIGURE

Spiral tube

[1] Using a #12 needle and a 2-yd. (1.8m) length of Nymo B or Fireline, pick up three 9º seed beads. Tie the beads into a circle with a square knot (Basics, p. 7), leaving a 14-in. (36cm) tail. Sew through the first bead on the circle. This is **Round 1**.

Round 2: Pick up a 14º and a 9º, and go through the next 9º on the circle. Repeat two times to complete the round (**figure, a–b**).

Round 3: Pick up two 14ºs and a 9º, and go through the first 9º on the previous round. Repeat two more times (**b–c**).

Round 4: Pick up three 14ºs and a 9º, and go through the first 9º on the previous round. Repeat two more times to complete the round (**c–d**).

[2] Repeat **Round 4** until the spiral measures approximately 7 in. (18cm).

[3] To end the spiral, repeat **Round 3**, and then **Round 2**. For the last round, stitch a 9º on each 9º on the previous round. Tie several half-hitch knots (Basics) between beads and leave a 14-in. tail. Don't trim the tail at the other end of the spiral.

[4] Repeat steps 1 and 2 to make two more spirals, one 1 in. (2.5cm) long and one 4 in. (10cm) long. End each spiral with **Round 4**, leaving the

working end untapered. Knot the working thread, secure it in the beadwork, and trim. Don't trim the 14-in. tail.

Gradated strands

The strands range from 17¼–18½ in. (44–47cm). Varying their length slightly makes them drape gracefully, and a slight variation of the position of each color change makes a subtle gradation. The rate of gradation is different on each side, with one side shifting colors more rapidly. Start with the shortest strand and make each subsequent strand one to three beads longer.

[1] Start with a 3-yd. (2.7m) length of Nymo D or Fireline and an extra-long beading needle. Position a stop bead (Basics) 2 in. (5cm) from the tail end.

[2] Work the short side with the shortest strand (18 in.). Pick up nine color A 11ºs, a 14º, an A 11º, a 14º, an A 11º, and 14 14ºs. Loop the thread twice through a soldered ring and tie a square knot. Then go back through all the strung beads except the stop bead (**photo a**). Remove the stop bead and tie a half-hitch knot (Basics) around the working thread with the tail.

Bring the tail back through a few more beads, tying half-hitch knots, and trim.

[3] To begin the gradation, pick up a color B 11º, 3 As, a B, two As, a B, an A, a B, an A, and eight or nine Bs. String the same gradation pattern with color C 11ºs. Continue the pattern using colors D through F. Then string about 2 in. (5cm) of Fs. This half of the strand is about 6¼ in. (16cm) long to the center of F beads.

[4] Work the gradation pattern in reverse, from color E to color A, stringing longer sections and changing colors every 1–1¼ in. This half of the strand is about 11 in. (28cm) long.

[5] After stringing the 14 14ºs, as in step two, loop the thread twice around the second soldered ring and secure it with a square knot. Leave some slack so the strand hangs nicely and is not stiff.

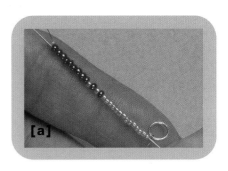

[a]

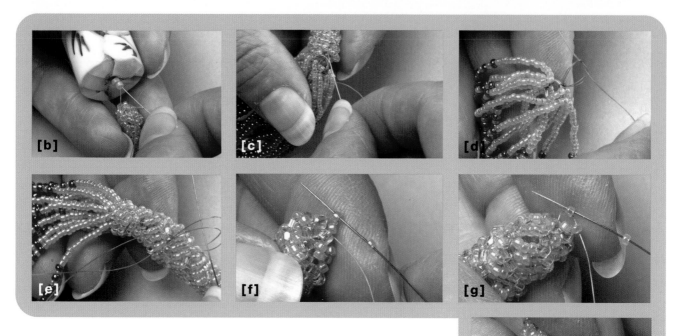

[6] As you work each subsequent strand, vary the number of beads within each gradation by one or two so each strand is slightly longer and the gradations don't line up. String a total of 14 graded strands.

Assembly

[1] Thread a long beading needle on the tail at the untapered end of the longest spiral and go through the art bead. Fill the inside of the art bead with 11ºs to keep it from shifting on the necklace (you'll need to go through these beads several times).

[2] Sew through the top beads of the 1-in. spiral (at the end with no tail) and go back through the 11ºs inside the art bead again (**photo b**). Sew through a few beads at the end of the long spiral and go back through the 11ºs inside the art bead. Repeat until the spirals are securely connected to the art bead. Then weave the thread into the beadwork, tie a few half-hitch knots between beads, and trim.

[3] Thread a needle on the tail of the 1-in. spiral. Weave through the beads of the spiral as needed to exit the center of the spiral. If the soldered ring doesn't fit inside the spiral, use chainnose pliers to form it into an oval. Go through the ring on the short end of the gradated strands twice and tie a square knot. Go back up the center of the spiral, pulling the ring inside the spiral so it doesn't

show (**photo c**). Sew through some of the beads at the top of the 1-in. spiral. Repeat this step a few times for strength.

[4] Start a doubled length of thread and tie it securely to the remaining split ring with a square knot (**photo d**). Glue the knot. Bring the needle up the 4-in. spiral, about 1 in., and ease the spiral down over the ring. Secure the thread between beads (**photo e**). Go down through the ring and then back up the spiral. Tie a few half-hitch knots between beads, and trim the thread.

[5] At one end of the necklace, thread the 14-in. starting tail on a beading needle. Pick up two 14ºs and go through the two top beads on the spiral. Pick up a 14º, skip the next 14º on the spiral, and go through the next (**photo f**).

[6] Turn, pick up a 14º, skip the first 14º, and go through the next (**photo g**). Continue working a two-bead peyote (Basics) strip for 6–8 rows. Bring the peyote strip through a soldered jump ring, and sew through the beads at the top of the spiral next to the strap (**photo h**). Reinforce the join of the peyote strip to the spiral a few times. Then end the thread.

[7] Repeat steps 5 and 6 on the other end of the necklace to attach the lobster claw clasp.

Elegant Victorian collar

Stitch a vintage reproduction necklace

by **Cheryl Assemi**

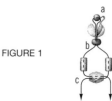

FIGURE 1

Draw your inspiration from the past—scour antique stores or art catalogs for designs—and recreate a classic with modern beads. Your result will be a timeless treasure.

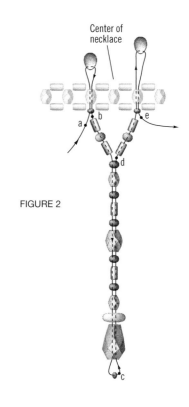

Center of necklace

FIGURE 2

Base

[1] Cut a 4-yd. (3.7m) length of Silamide and thread a needle at each end. String a 15º color A seed bead to the center of the thread. Pass both needles through a bead tip and an 11º color A seed bead (**figure 1, a–b**).

[2] String a bugle bead on each thread and cross through a 3mm fire-polished bead (**b–c**). Repeat 76 times, or until the necklace is 16 in. (41cm) long.

[3] String a bugle on each thread and pass both needles through an 11º A and a bead tip. Cross through a 15º A and back through the bead tip. Carefully repeat the thread path on the entire piece to reinforce it. Tie a surgeon's knot (Basics, p. 7) in the first bead tip. Glue the knot and trim the tails.

Bugle points and fringe

[1] Thread a needle with 4 yd. of Silamide. String a 15º color B seed bead to the center of the thread and pass up through the crystal to the left of the middle crystal on the base. (Set aside the other half of thread.) Add a tiny teardrop and pass back through the 3mm and the 15º B (**figure 2, a–b**).

[2] Pick up a bugle, an 11º color C, a bugle, an 11º A, and a 3mm.

[3] Pick up an 11º A, a bugle, an 11º A, a 4mm fire polished bead, an 11º A, a bugle, an 11º A, a 3mm, a flat spacer, a 7 x 5mm drop, and a 15º A (**b–c**).

[4] Sew back through the crystal drop and retrace the thread path through the first 11º A strung in step 2 (**c–d**).

[5] Pick up a bugle, an 11º C, a bugle, and a 15º B. Working to the right, skip a 3mm on the base and sew through the next 3mm. Pick up a tiny teardrop and sew back through the 3mm and the 15º B (**d–e**).

[6] Repeat step 2 (**figure 3, a–b**). Pick up an 11º A, two bugles, an 11º A, a 3 mm, a flat spacer, a 7 x 5mm drop, and a 15º A (**b–c**). Repeat steps 4 (**c–d**) and 5 (**d–e**).

[7] Repeat step 2 (**figure 4, a–b**). Pick up an 11º A, a 3mm, a flat spacer, a 7 x 5mm drop, and a 15º A (**b–c**). Repeat steps 4 and 5 (**c–d**).

[8] Repeat step 2. Pick up a flat spacer (**figure 5, a–b**), a 4mm, and a 15º A (**b–c**). Retrace the thread path to the 11º A and repeat step 5 (**c–d**).

[9] Repeat step 2. Pick up a 15º A and retrace the thread path to the 11º A. Repeat step 5. Do this 15 times or until you reach the end of the necklace. On the last fringe come up through the 11º A and the bead tip.

Go through the 15º A in the bead tip, then pass back through the bead tip, the 11º A, and the lower bugle. Go up through the end 3mm, string a tiny teardrop, and go back through the 3mm (**figure 6**). Set the thread aside.

[10] Turn the necklace over and thread a needle on the 2 yd. (1.8m) tail from step 1. Repeat steps 6–9 on the other half of the necklace.

[11] Working with the thread on the left end of the necklace, pick up three 15º color C seed beads. *Sew down through the 11º A between the bugle beads (**a–b**). String *three 15º C, an 11º A, a 3mm, and a 15º A (**figure 7, b–c**). Sew back through the 3mm and the 11º A. String *three 15º Cs

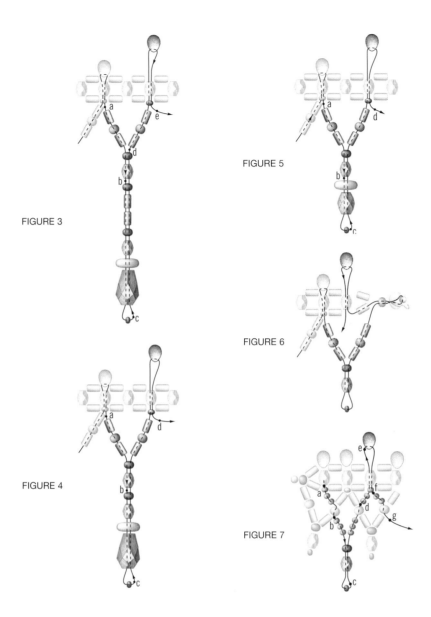

FIGURE 3

FIGURE 4

FIGURE 5

FIGURE 6

FIGURE 7

MATERIALS

necklace 18 in. (46cm)

- **5** 7 x 5mm drops Czech fire-polished glass beads, gold lined
- **3** 4mm Czech fire-polished glass beads, gold lined
- **163** 3mm Czech fire-polished glass beads, gold lined
- **79** tiny teardrop beads, purple iris
- **247** 3mm Japanese bugle beads, purple iris
- **2g** each of size 11º Japanese seed beads:
  metallic gold, color A
  gold-lined crystal, color C
- size 15º Japanese seed beads:
  2g metallic gold, color A
  2g purple iris, color B
  10g gold-lined crystal, color C
- **6** 4mm flat spacers, gold
- clasp
- **2** bead tips
- Silamide thread
- beading needles, #13
- G-S Hypo Cement

Tools: chainnose pliers, roundnose pliers

and sew up through the 11º A between the bugle beads to the right (**c–d**). String three 15º Cs, and sew through the 3mm on the base (**d–e**). Pick up a tiny teardrop and sew back through the 3mm and the last 15º C (**e–f**). Pick up two 15º Cs and sew through the next 11º A (**f–g**). Repeat (**b–g**) until you've added fifteen 15ºs, three-bead fringes.

[12] Repeat step 11, but string four 15º Cs at each *. Do this two times.

[13] Repeat step 11, but string five 15º Cs at each *.

[14] Repeat step 11, but string six 15º Cs at each *. Now you are at the center of the necklace. Weave the tail back through the base and tie it off with a couple of half-hitch

knots (Basics) between beads. Trim the tail.

[15] Turn the necklace and repeat steps 11–14. When you reach the center, skip the tiny teardrop already in place and carefully weave the tail back through the base occasionally tying half-hitch knots between beads. Trim the tail.

Finishing

[1] Thread a needle to the center of 1½ yd. (1.4m) of Silamide. To hold the tiny teardrops in place, run the doubled thread through the top row of bugles and tiny teardrops. Knot off the tails in the bead tips with a surgeon's knot, dab the knot with glue, and trim the ends.

[2] Repeat step 1 with the lower line of bugles and 15º B. Close the bead tips with the chainnose pliers.

[3] With the roundnose pliers, attach the hook on each bead tip to a loop on the clasp.

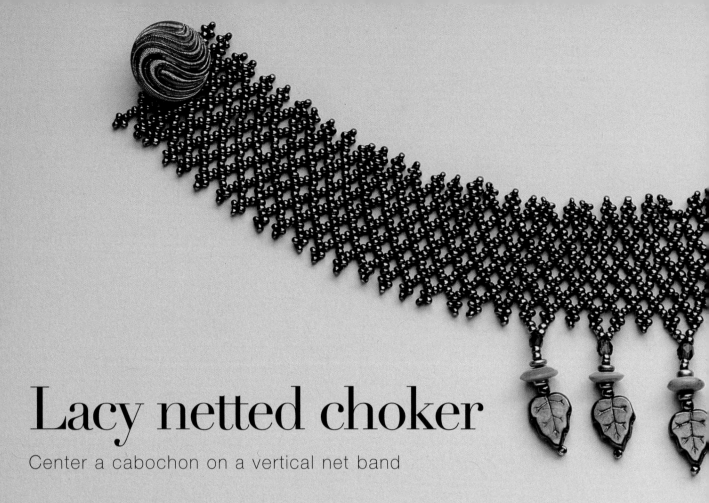

Lacy netted choker

Center a cabochon on a vertical net band

by **Paula Marie Walter**

Back the cabochon

[1] Begin the centerpiece by gluing the cabochon to the center of a 3-in. (7.6cm) square of Lacy's Stiff Stuff with E6000 adhesive. Place the Lacy's on a piece of wax paper (cab side up) and cover it with a soft cloth. Weight it down with a heavy book and allow it to dry completely overnight. Allow the back to air dry if it's still wet, then remove any excess glue from around the cab with a toothpick.

[2] Start a 45-in (1.1m) length of conditioned thread, and tie a large knot at the end. Pierce a hole through the backing next to the cabochon.

[3] Leaving a 6-in. (15cm) tail, come up through the hole from the underside. Step one bead's width away and go back down right against the stone. Tie the tail and working thread together with a square knot (Basics, p. 7 and **photo a**, p. 46). Glue the knot. Come back up one of the holes, and tie a couple of half-hitch knots around the thread between the holes. Go back down through one of the holes, and tie the working thread to the tail with another square knot. Glue the knot.

[4] Come back up through the hole as close to the stone as possible.

Backstitch

[1] To begin backstitch, pick up three seed beads and place them next to the cabochon. Sew down through the backing just past the third bead (**photo b**).

[2] Come back up through the first hole and go through the three beads again to reinforce them.

[3] Pick up three more beads, position them against the edge of the stone, and sew through the backing just past the last bead. Come up between the third and fourth beads (**photo c**) and go through the last three beads again. Repeat this step until you have encircled the stone. You may need to adjust the number of beads in the last few stitches. End with an even number of beads.

[4] Sew through the ring of beads to reinforce it.

Create the bezel

Work the bezel in circular even-count peyote (Basics), using the backstitch row as the starting ring. Most cabochons will only need two rounds of peyote, but some have a high dome and may need four to six rounds. For a tight fit, decrease as needed at the corners or curves.

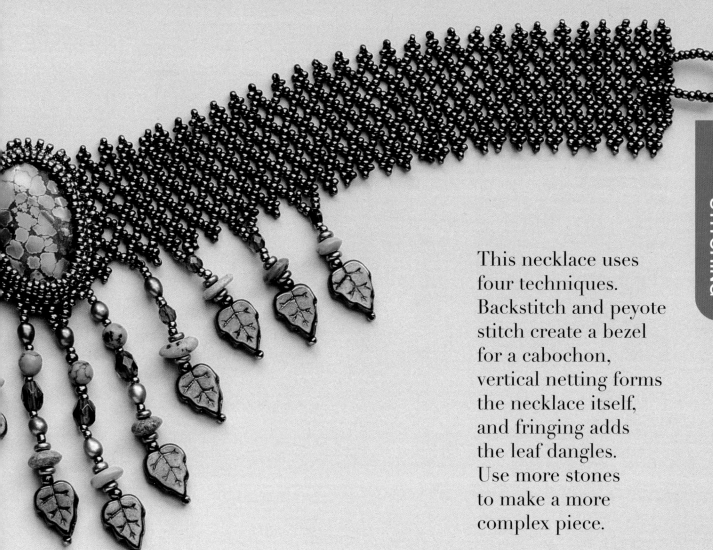

This necklace uses four techniques. Backstitch and peyote stitch create a bezel for a cabochon, vertical netting forms the necklace itself, and fringing adds the leaf dangles. Use more stones to make a more complex piece.

[1] With your needle exiting a bead on the backstitch row, pick up a bead, skip a bead, and go through the next bead. Continue around the circle. Step up by sewing through the first bead of this round (Basics).

[2] Reinforce the bezel by sewing through all the beads of the last two rows again (**photo d**).

[3] Sew down between the bezel and the cabochon and through the backing. Tie a few half-hitch knots on the stitches on the back and trim the thread.

[4] Trim the excess backing as close to the beads as you can without snipping a thread. Glue the back of the cabochon to a second piece of Lacy's and let it dry. Then trim the second backing as you did the first.

Edge the bezel

[1] With the edge of the backing sitting at a right angle to the bezel, sew down under the backstitch row and bring the needle out between the two pieces of Lacy's.

[2] Pick up three beads, skip one bead's width, and bring the needle through both pieces of Lacy's, near the edge. Sew back through the third bead (**figure 1**) and pull gently to position the beads as shown.

[3] Pick up two beads and bring the needle from back to front through the Lacy's (**photo e**). Go back through the second bead (**figure 2**). Repeat this step around the bezel until you are a bead's width away from the first edging bead.

[4] Pick up a bead and go down the first bead and the Lacy's. Then sew back through the first and second beads (**figure 3**). Tie a few half-hitch knots around threads between beads and trim the thread.

Stitch the neck band

[1] Center a needle on a 3-yd. (2.7m) length of conditioned thread. String a stop bead (Basics) to 15 in. (38cm) from the thread ends.

MATERIALS

- 20 x 30mm cabochon
- accent beads (approx. 4–8mm)
- hank size 11º seed beads
- Silamide or Nymo D
- beeswax or Thread Heaven
- beading needles, #12 Sharps
- 2 3-in. squares of Lacy's Stiff Stuff (LacysStiffStuff.com)
- E6000 adhesive

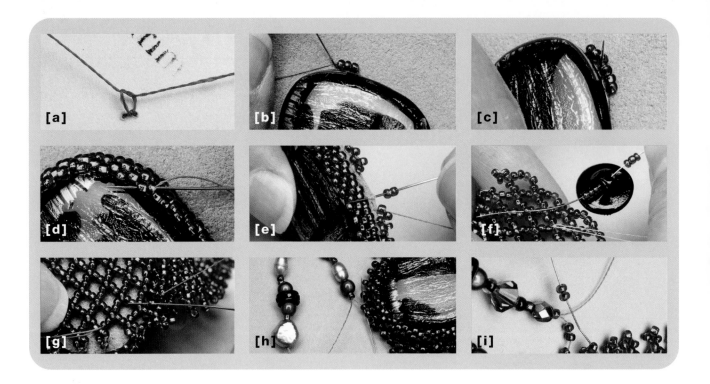

[a] [b] [c]
[d] [e] [f]
[g] [h] [i]

[2] Work the netted band as follows:
Row 1: Pick up 22 beads. Skipping the last three beads, go back through the fourth bead from the end toward the start (**figure 4, a–b**).
Row 2: Pick up five beads, skip five beads, and go through the sixth bead (**b-c**). Repeat two more times. End the row with a picot: Pick up six beads and go through the fourth (**d–e**).
Row 3: Pick up five beads and go through the fifth bead on the previous row (**e–f**). Repeat two more times (**f–g**). End the row with a picot (**g–h**).
[3] Continue stitching rows of netting until you reach the desired length of the necklace. End the last row without a picot.

Attach the clasp
[1] Retrace the thread path and exit the bead above the center net on the next-to-last row.
[2] String two or three beads, the button, and two or three beads. Sew through the bead below the center net as shown in **photo f**. Retrace the thread path a few times, secure the thread in the beadwork, and trim.
[3] Remove the stop bead, thread a needle on the tail, and repeat step 1.
[4] Pick up enough beads to make a loop around the button. Connect

the loop to the netting as in step 2, reinforce the beads, and trim.
[5] Sew the cabochon to the center of the choker by stitching between beads in the netting and the Lacy's until the cabochon is secured around the edges (**photo g**).

Add the fringe
[1] Start a new length of thread and secure it at the center bottom edge of the cabochon. String the beads for the longest fringe and end with a seed bead. Skip the seed bead at the bottom of the fringe and go back through all the other fringe beads. Sew into the other side of the edge bead so the fringe hangs below it (**photo h**).
[2] Weave through the edge beads to the third bead after the center fringe. String the next fringe slightly shorter than the first.
[3] Sew through to the center bead on the picot. String a bridge of one or two seed beads then the fringe beads. Go back through the fringe beads and string the same number of bridge beads. Then go into the center bead of the next picot (**photo i**). Add three more picot fringes, skipping a picot between fringes.
[4] Repeat steps 2–4 on the other side of the center fringe.

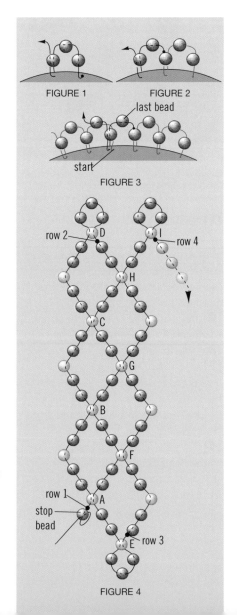

FIGURE 1   FIGURE 2

last bead

start

FIGURE 3

row 2 — D   I — row 4

H

C   G

B   F

row 1
stop
bead   A

E — row 3

FIGURE 4

Mesh motifs

Stitch fast and versatile
geometric panels into a choker

by **Marilyn K. Lowe**

Netting is one of the fastest and easiest off-loom bead stitches. You can create an almost infinite array of patterns by changing bead colors and net sizes and shapes. This choker incorporates colorful diamond patterns on lacy panels.

Determine the length

[1] Determine the finished length of your necklace and subtract 1½–2 in. (3.8–5cm) for finishing the ends. This necklace measures 18 in. (46cm) and consists of 13 large motifs and 16 small ones.

[2] Using a 5-yd. (4.6m) length of conditioned thread (Basics, p. 7) doubled, string a stop bead (Basics) to 6 in. (15cm) from the end.

Large motif

Rows 1 and **2** (first motif only):
a. Pick up 14 color A seed beads, a color B, and an A. Go back through the eighth bead from the needle (**figure 1, a–b**).
b. Pick up three As, skip three As on the first row, and go through the fourth A (**b–c**).
c. Pick up a B, a C, and a B and go through the first A in **Row 1** (**c–d**).
Row 3 (**d–e**): a. Pick up two Cs, an A, a B, and go through the C.

b. Pick up a B, two As, and go through the A.
c. Pick up two As, a B, and go through the B.
First picot (**e–f**): Pick up a B, six As, a C, three Bs, and through C and last A added.
b. Pick up two As and go through 13th and 14th As in **Row 1** and first B and three As of this picot.
Row 4 (**f–g**): a. Three As, two Bs, and go through the first A of the picot.
b. A, C, A, through A.
c. Two Bs, A, through A.
d. Three As, through A.
Row 5 (**g–h**): a. Two Cs, two As, through A.
b. Two As, B, through B.
c. B, two Cs, through C.
d. Two Cs, B, through B.
Second picot (**h–i**): B, six As, C, three Bs, through C and last A added.
b. Two As, through the second and third A in Row 4 and first B and three As of this picot.

Row 6 (**i-j**): a. Three As, two Bs, through A.
b. A, two Cs, through C.
c. A, B, A, through C.
d. Two Cs, A, through A.
e. Two Bs, A, through A.
Row 7 (**j-k**): a. Two Cs, two As, through B.
b. B, two As, through C.
c. Two Cs, A, through B.
d. A, two Cs, through C.
e. Two As, B, through B.
Center picot (**k-l**): a. Six As, C, five Bs, through C and last A added.
b. Three As and through the second and third A in **Row 6** and the first two As of the picot.
Row 8 (**l-m**): a. Three As, through A.
b. Three Bs, through C.
c. Three Cs, through C.
d. Three Bs, through A.
e. Three As, through A.
Row 9 (**m-n**): a. Two Cs, two As, through A.
b. Three As, through B.

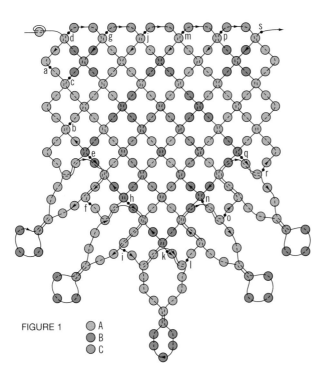

FIGURE 1

○ A
● B
○ C

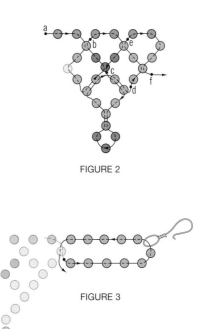

FIGURE 2

FIGURE 3

c. B, two As, through C.

d. Two As, B, through B.

Fourth picot (n–o): a. Five As, C, three Bs, through C and last A added.

b. Two As, through the second and third A in **Row 8**, next A, next B, and first two As of this picot.

Row 10 (o–p): a. Three As, through A.

b. Three Bs, through A.

c. Three Bs, through A.

d. B, C, B, through A.

Row 11 (p–q): a. Two Cs, A, B, through C.

b. B, two As, through A.

c. Three As, through B.

Fifth picot (q–r): a. Five As, C, three B, through C and last A added.

b. Two As, through the second and third A in **Row 10**, next A, next B, and first two As of this picot.

Row 12 (r–s): Three As, through A. Repeat twice.

Small motif

Row 1 (figure 2, a–b): a. Two Cs, two As, through corresponding A on large motif 's edge row.

b. Three As, two Bs, through first A in this row.

Row 2 (b–c): Two Cs, A, B, through B.

Picot (c–d): a. Four As, C, three Bs, through C and last A added.

b. A, through the last two As of **Row 1** and the first two As of this picot.

Row 3 (d–e): Three As, through A.

Row 4 (e–f): Two Cs, two As, through A.

Note: to stitch a large motif after a small one, start at **figure 2, point f** and pick up 11 As instead of 14.

MATERIALS

necklace 18 in. (46cm)

- 10g size 11º Czech seed beads, in each of 3 colors: A, B, C
- Nymo B conditioned with beeswax
- beading needles, #13
- clasp
- G-S Hypo Cement

Clasp

[1] Go through the last two nets stitched in the small motif and exit at the first A in the last row of the small motif.

[2] Pick up 11 As and the clasp loop, tighten the beads, and go through the A from step 1 again. Go through the loop again to reinforce it (**figure 3**).

[3] Secure the thread in the beadwork with half-hitch knots (Basics). Seal the knots with glue and trim.

[4] Repeat on the other end of the necklace.

Crystal fringe choker

Combine bead stringing, right-angle weave, and fringe in this versatile necklace design

by **Linda Richmond**

Two rows of right-angle weave establish the base for a sophisticated fringe that falls at the front of these necklaces. Leaf beads lend a casual feel to the necklace, while dagger beads create a dressier version.

Necklace base

[1] Cut a piece of beading wire 6 in. (15cm) longer than the desired necklace length, and clamp or tape the wire 3 in. (7.6cm) from one end. String a color A 11º seed bead, a color B 11º seed bead, an A 11º, and a B 11º.

[2] String a color A cathedral bead, an A 11º, a color B cathedral bead, an A 11º, an A cathedral, a crystal, a 6mm color C cathedral bead, and a crystal. Repeat this pattern once. Then string an A cathedral, an A 11º, a B cathedral, an A 11º, an A cathedral, and two A 11ºs.

[3] For the base of the right-angle weave section, string an alternating pattern of B 11ºs and A 11ºs for a total of 101 beads.

[4] String the other end of the necklace as in steps 1 and 2, but reverse the order of the beads. After stringing the last 11º, clamp or tape the wire about ⅛ in. (3mm) from the last bead to allow ease for the right-angle weave.

Right-angle weave

[1] Center a needle on 2½ yd. (2.3m) of conditioned thread (Basics, p. 7), and use the thread doubled.

[2] Go through the fifth bead before the 11ºs, and secure the thread with several half-hitch knots between beads (Basics). Glue the knots. Exit through the first B 11º (**figure 1, point a**).

[3] Work in right-angle weave for steps 3–5, using 11ºs as follows: Pick up an A, a B, and an A, and go back through the B on the base row (**a–b**). Continue through the first A added (**b–c**). Pick up a B and an A, go through the next B on the base, and continue through all the beads of the second stitch (**c–d**).

[4] Go through the next B on the base (**d–e**). Pick up an A and a B, and go through the A at the edge of the second stitch. Continue through the same B on the base and the next A (**e–f**). Work in right-angle weave across the row, ending with the B.

[5] Begin the second row with your thread exiting at **figure 2, point a**. Go through the B at the bottom of the stitch, pick up an A, a B, and an A, and go back through the B on the

previous row (**a–b**). Continue through the next A. Pick up a B and an A, and go back through the next three beads on this stitch (**b–c**). Work in right-angle weave across the row.

Fringe

[1] Anchor a 3-yd. (2.7m) thread in the necklace base, and use it doubled. Exit the bottom B 11º of the far left stitch (**figure 3, point a**).

[2] For the dagger necklace, pick up an A 11º, a B 11º, an A 11º, a crystal, a color A disk bead, a color C 8mm or 6mm cathedral, a B 11º, four A 11ºs, a dagger, and four A 11ºs. Go back through the B 11º, the 8mm or 6mm, the disk, and the crystal. Pick up an A 11º, a B 11º, and an A 11º. Skip the second right-angle weave stitch. Go through the bottom bead on the third stitch (**a–b**).

[3] For the leaf necklace, pick up a B 11º, an A 11º, a B 11º, a crystal, an A 11º, a disk, an A 11º, a color C 8mm or 6mm cathedral, an A 11º, a B 11º, an A 11º, a leaf, an A 11º, a B 11º, and an A 11º. Go back through the B 11º, the 8mm or 6mm, the A 11º, the disk, the A 11º, and the crystal. Pick up a B 11º, an A 11º, and a B 11º. Skip the second right-angle weave stitch. Go through the bottom bead on the third stitch.

[4] After completing the 25th fringe, secure the thread in the necklace base.

Finishing

[1] Remove the clamp or tape from the beading wire. Add or remove beads on the necklace base to adjust the length as desired.

[2] On one end, string a crimp bead and one half of the clasp. Go back through the crimp bead and the first four 11ºs, tighten the wire, crimp the crimp bead (Basics), and trim the wire. Repeat on the other end.

Editor's note: When 6 in. (15cm) of thread remains, secure it in the beadwork with three or four half-hitch knots between beads. Don't place the knots before or after the bottom bead on any stitch.

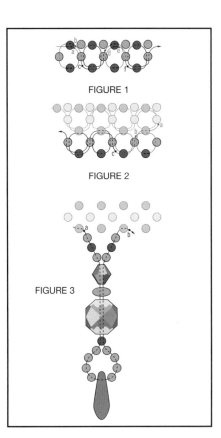

FIGURE 1

FIGURE 2

FIGURE 3

STITCHING

MATERIALS

necklace 15½ in. (39.4cm)

- cathedral beads
  25 8mm (or 6mm), color C
  12 6mm, color A
  6 6mm, color B
  4 6mm, color C
- **25** top-drilled leaf beads or daggers
- **33** 4mm bicone crystals, color B
- **25** 4mm disk beads, color A
- 15g size 11º Japanese seed beads in each of 2 colors: A, B
- toggle clasp
- **2** crimp beads
- Nymo B conditioned with beeswax
- flexible beading wire, .012–.014
- beading needles, #12
- G-S Hypo Cement

Tools: chainnose or crimping pliers, wire cutters, clamps

Floral fantasy

Embellish a single strand with glass beads, crystals, and pearls

by **Bindy Lambell**

Look through your stash of leftover beads before you start. You'll likely find many beads that are perfect for the fringe ends. As you work, vary the lengths of the fringe for fullness, but keep the fringe short enough so the base doesn't stand out.

Necklace

[1] Cut a 32-in. (81cm) length of flexible beading wire. Determine the finished length of your necklace minus the length of the clasp. String 8° triangle or seed beads on the beading wire until you reach the desired length. Center the beads on the wire.

[2] Tape the beading wire next to the first and last beads. Then clamp hemostats on each piece of tape to hold the beads on the wire (**photo a**). You'll add fringe between these beads, so the 8°s should not be snug against each other. As you work, adjust the spacing between the beads by moving the tape and hemostats at either end.

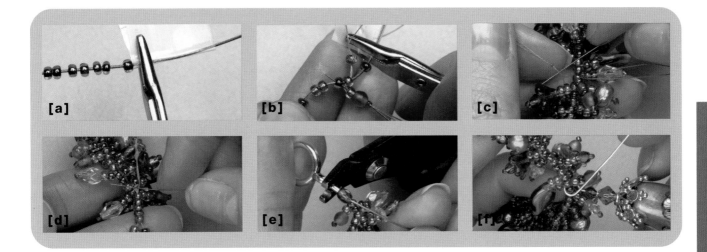

[a] [b] [c]

[d] [e] [f]

[3] Thread a needle with a 2-yd. (1.8m) length of Silamide. Using the thread doubled, string a stop bead (Basics, p. 7) 6 in. (15cm) from the end of the thread.

[4] Go through the end bead on the strand and string an 8º, an accent bead, and an 11º. Skip the 11º and go back through the accent bead, the 8º, and the next 8º on the wire (photo b).

[5] Continue adding fringe between each 8º. To add beads with holes across the top, string two or three 8ºs, the bead, and two or three 8ºs. Go through the next 8º on the wire. Each fringe should be less than ¾ in. (1.9cm) long.

[6] Remove the stop bead, tie off the doubled thread at each end with front-back-front knots (Basics), and trim the tails.

[7] Divide the necklace length into thirds. Add a second row of fringe to the middle section, working from one end of the section to the other. Start a new double length of thread and tie a knot at the end. Make a loop around the wire between two 8ºs by wrapping the thread around the wire and passing the needle between the threads (photo c). Bring the needle through the next 8º on the wire.

[8] This fringe should be slightly longer than the fringe in step 5, but not longer than 1¼ in. (3.2cm). String five 8ºs, an accent bead, and an 11º for longer fringe. For leaf fringe, string seven 8ºs, a leaf, and two 8ºs. Skipping the two 8ºs above the leaf, go back through the first five 8ºs, and the next 8º on the wire (photo d).

[9] Remove the tape and hemostat from one end of the wire. String an accent bead, a crimp bead, and a clasp half. Bring the wire back through the crimp bead and the accent bead. Crimp the crimp bead (Basics and photo e) and trim the tail. Repeat with the remaining wire end.

Dangle

[1] Cut a piece of 22-gauge wire 4 in. (10cm) longer than your focal bead. Make a loop at one end (Basics).

[2] String a 4mm crystal, a 6mm crystal, a bead cap, the focal bead, a bead cap, a 6mm crystal, and a 4mm crystal. Make the first half of a wrapped loop (Basics). Open the loop slightly and attach it to the center of the necklace (photo f). Finish the wraps and trim the excess wire.

[3] Thread a needle with a 1½-yd. (1.4m) length of Silamide. Center an 11º, an accent bead, and ten 8ºs on the thread. Thread a second needle on the tail. Skipping the 11º, pass through the accent bead and retrace the thread path to the last 8º strung. Bring both needles through the loop below the focal bead and back through the 8º both threads exit. Tie a front-back-front knot and remove both needles. Thread one needle on both threads and add fringe between each 8º as in steps 4 and 5. Tie the tails with front-back-front knots and trim the excess thread.

MATERIALS
necklace 27½ in. (69.9cm)
- focal bead (Bindy Lambell, bindy.com)
- **2** sterling silver bead caps (to fit the focal bead)
- **2** 6mm bicone crystals
- **2** 4mm bicone crystals
- **450–500** assorted accent beads, leaves, pearls, crystals, flowers, and seed beads
- hank size 8º seed beads or 50g size 8º triangles
- hank size 11º seed beads
- 8 in. (20cm) 22-gauge sterling silver wire
- crimp beads
- toggle clasp
- flexible beading wire, .019 or .024
- Silamide to match bead color
- beading needles, #12

Tools: chainnose pliers, crimping pliers, roundnose pliers, wire cutter, hemostats

3-D triangle weave necklace

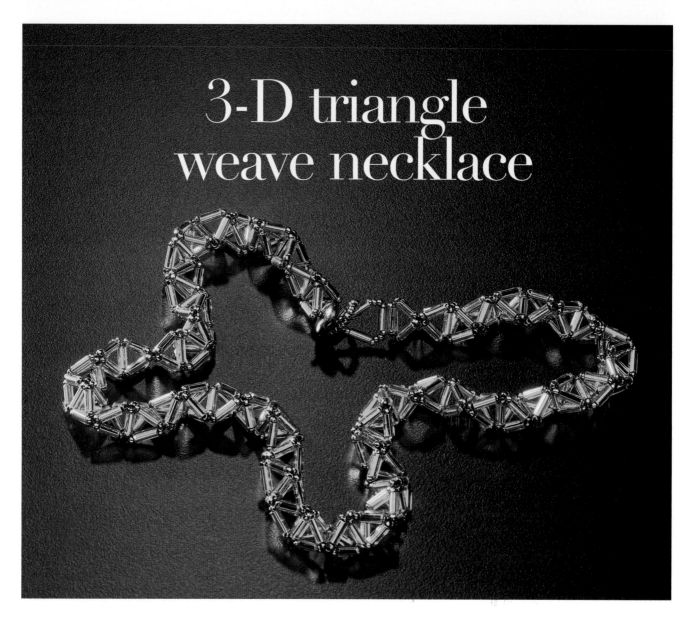

Stitch triangle weave in three dimensions

by **Tina Czuba**

Although similar to right-angle weave, this 3-D variation of triangle weave has its own distinct traits. One surprising feature is its unusual movement, which is similar to a series of opposing hinges.

[1] Thread a needle with a 2-yd. (1.8m) length of conditioned Nymo. Pick up a 15º seed bead, a bugle, two 15ºs, a bugle, two 15ºs, a bugle, and a 15º. Leaving an 8-in. (20cm) tail, go through all the beads again to form a triangle. Sew through the first 15º, bugle, and 15º again (figure 1).

[2] String a 15º, a bugle, two 15ºs, a bugle, and a 15º. Sew through the three beads on the previous triangle and the first three beads on the new triangle, exiting in the same direction (figure 2).

[3] Pick up a 15º, a bugle, and a 15º. Sew through the corresponding side of the first triangle (figure 3, a–b). Tighten the thread to create a pyramid. This is a 3-D unit.

[4] Pick up a 15º, a bugle, two 15ºs, a bugle, and a 15º. Sew through the same side of the first triangle as you did in the previous step (b–c).

[5] Repeat step 4. You now have two triangles sharing a side, or base, as in figure 2.

[6] Sew through the next side on either of these two triangles so your

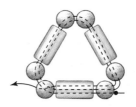

FIGURE 1

FIGURE 2

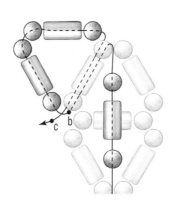

FIGURE 3

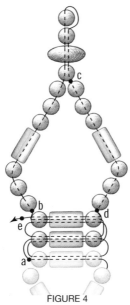

FIGURE 4

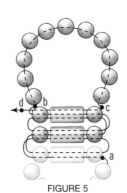

FIGURE 5

thread exits between 15ºs at the triangle's apex. Repeat step 3.

[7] Sew through the two adjoining sides of the triangle, so thread exits the beads that will become the base for the next 3-D unit.

[8] Repeat steps 4–7 until you reach the desired length.

[9] With your thread exiting the base of the last 3-D unit, pick up a 15º, a bugle, and a 15º. Sew back through the base row and the beads just added. Pick up a 15º, a bugle, and a 15º. Sew through the previous row and back through the beads just added (figure 4, a–b).

[10] To make the button end of the clasp, string three 15ºs, a bugle, four 15ºs, a rondelle, and two 15ºs.

Skip the last 15º, and go back through the next 15º, rondelle, and 15º (b–c). Pick up three 15ºs, a bugle, and three 15ºs (c–d). Weave through the 15º, bugle, and 15º (d–e). Secure the thread in the beadwork and trim.

[11] For the clasp loop, thread the needle onto the tail from step 1. Work a ladder of seed beads and bugles as in step 7 (figure 5, a–b).

[12] Pick up enough 15ºs to make a loop that fits over the rondelle (b–c). Sew through the last row of the ladder (c–d) and the loop of beads again to reinforce them. Secure the threads and trim the tails.

Editor's note: You can make this necklace with larger beads without changing the directions.

MATERIALS

- 25g 3mm bugle beads
- 10g size 15º seed beads
- 12–18mm rondelle or small button for clasp
- Nymo B to match bead color
- beeswax or Thread Heaven
- beading needles, #13

Totally tubular

Stitch an awesome necklace using Dutch spiral and bugle beads

by **JoAnn Allard**

Open up a traditional Dutch spiral by using bugle beads and small spacers. You can experiment with a monochromatic color scheme or use multiple hues to highlight the shape. The open weave created by the bugle beads makes a fun tubular shape.

[1] Measure 3 yd. (2.7m) of flexible beading wire. Do not cut it from the spool. String an E bead, a bugle, an E, a bugle, an E, and a bugle; slide the beads to the spool. Pass the wire through the first E bead to make a circle (**photo a**).

[2] Pick up an E bead and a bugle. Go through the second E from step 1 (**photo b**). Pick up an E and a bugle and go through the last E from step 1. Continue adding Es and bugles, going through the Es on the previous row, until the piece measures 4½ in. (11.4cm) long. This is the end of the first section.

[3] Measure 3 yd. of flexible beading wire from the spool and cut it off. Now resume stitching from the center of the necklace until the entire length is 9 in. (23cm). Noting where you stopped the design, work the wire end into the beadwork, tie a half-hitch knot (Basics, p. 7) next to an E, and go through a few beads. Make another knot and go through a few beads; trim.

[4] Using a twisted wire needle, attach a 2 yd. (1.8m) length of nylon bead cord securely to one end of the beadwork, exiting the same bead you exited in the previous section.

[5] Pick up an E and seven 11º seed beads. (The seed beads replace the bugles in the previous section.) Go through the next E in the previous row (**photo c**).

[6] Pick up an E and seven 11ºs and go through the next E in the previous row. Repeat this step one more time.

[7] Continue as in step 5, but pick up six 11º seed beads instead of seven for a full row. Continue in this manner. For each round, string one less seed bead per section until you reach three seed beads.

[8] Continue stitching, using three seeds instead of the bugles, until the entire seed bead section is 4 in. (10cm) long. Exit an E (**figure, a–b**).

[9] Pick up 21 11º seed beads (**b–c**). Go through the next E (**c–d**).

[10] Pick up ten 11ºs and go through the 11th 11º from step 9 (**d–e**). Pick up ten more 11ºs and go through the next E (**e–f**).

[11] Go through a few beads, securing the thread with half-hitch knots (Basics), and trim the tail.

[12] Trim the head of a head pin and make the first half of a wrapped loop (Basics) on one end. Attach the seed-bead loops and finish the wrap (**photo d**). String a cone over the wrapped loop. Make the first half of a wrapped loop right above the cone, attach the clasp half, and finish the wraps. Repeat from step 4 on the other end of the necklace.

MATERIALS
- **195** #5 bugles
- **414** E-beads or 4mm druks
- 10g size 11º seed beads
- flexible beading wire, .014
- nylon bead cord such as Strength #2
- twisted wire needles
- **2** head pins or 2 in. pieces of 24-gauge wire
- 2⅝-in. (6.7cm) cones
- clasp

Tools: chainose pliers, roundnose pliers, wire cutters

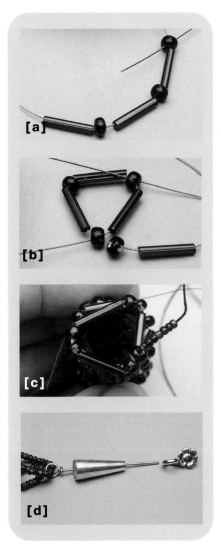

[a]

[b]

[c]

[d]

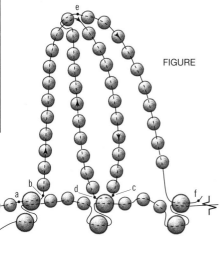

FIGURE

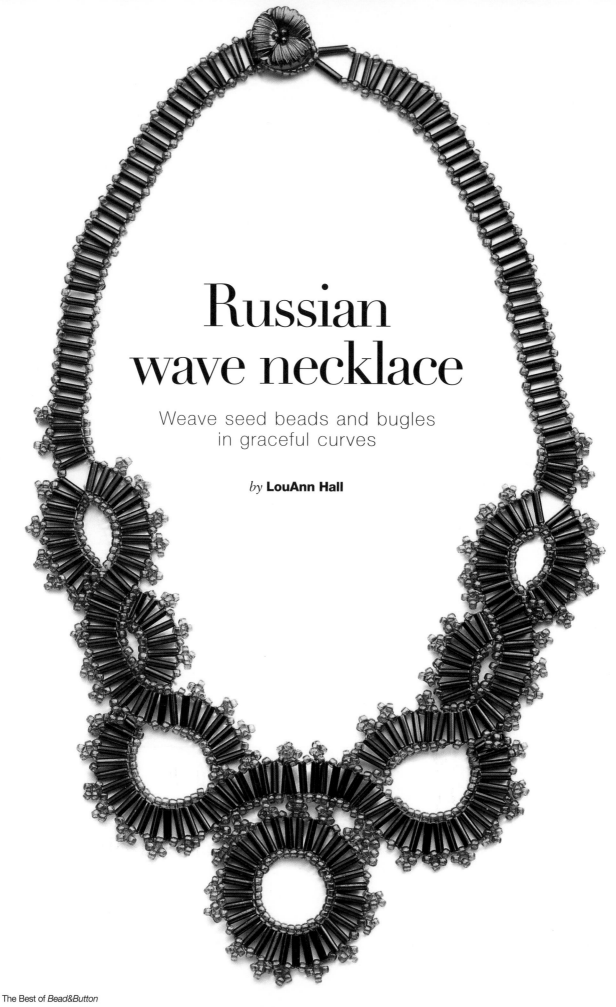

Russian wave necklace

Weave seed beads and bugles
in graceful curves

by **LouAnn Hall**

This necklace is made using a technique known in Russian as *zhyabo*, which translates to jabot, meaning ornamental frill or bit of lace. American beaders call the technique Russian wave because of its curves. A Russian wave design is composed of several elements— a basic element, a circle, and an S-shaped curve—made with bugle and seed beads and connected to each other.

Make the elements

Basic element

[1] String two needles on a 2-yd. (1.8m) length of thread and tie the ends together with an overhand knot (Basics, p. 7), leaving a 3–4-in. (7.6–10cm) tail. Seal the knot with glue. Then center the knot between the needles and slide them as far apart as possible.

[2] With the right-hand needle, pick up a bugle bead, an 11º, and a bugle. Slide them next to the knot. Sew through the first bugle again in the same direction and tighten the thread. Continue through the 11º and the second bugle (**figure 1**).

[3] With the left-hand needle, pick up an 11º and go through the second bugle (**figure 2**). The 11ºs on this side of the ladder form the spine. The needles have switched places.

[4] With the right-hand needle, pick up an 11º and a bugle. Go through the previous bugle and the new 11º and tighten the thread (**figure 3, a–b**). Pick up three 11ºs and go through the first 11º added in this step in the same direction to form a picot unit (**b–c**). Go through the new bugle (**c–d**).

[5] With the left-hand needle, pick up an 11º, and go through the end bugle (**figure 4**).

[6] Continue building the basic element, alternating between standard (one-bead) and picot (four-bead) units on the right-hand edge until you have strung ten bugles (five standard and four picot units).

[7] Finish a basic element with a standard unit. The top needle has passed through the last bugle toward the left. Run it through all the spine beads (**figure 5, a–b**). The bottom needle, which added the last spine bead, is on the right. Run it through the last standard unit seed, the next-to-last bugle, and the last spine bead

(**c–d**). Bury the starting tail in the beadwork, but leave the needles and working threads in place.

[8] Make a second ten-bugle element. Then make two eight-bugle elements (four standard units and three picots).

Circular element

[1] Repeat step 1 above but start with a 4-yd. (3.7m) length of thread.

[2] Follow steps 2–6 above, and continue alternating standard and picot elements until you have a total of 32 bugles, ending with the 16th standard unit.

[3] Pick up an 11º on the right-hand needle (the thread exits the outer edge) and go through the first bugle from the outer to the inner edge (**figure 6, a–b**). Go up the last bugle and continue through the 11º (**b–c**). String three 11ºs and make a picot (**c–d**). Go through the first bugle again (**d–e**).

[4] With the left-hand needle, which is exiting the last bugle toward the inside, pick up a spine 11º and go through the first bugle (**f–g**). Secure this thread in the beadwork, glue the knots, and trim off the excess thread.

[5] With the first needle (**point e**), go through the spine beads on the inside of the circle. Tighten so the beads lie flat. End this thread, glue the knots, and trim the excess. Weave in the tail.

Side S element

[1] Make a basic element with 12 bugles. To make the curve reverse, turn the piece over and follow the directions for a basic element, starting with a standard unit, for another 12 bugles (six more picots). There will be a total of 24 bugles. Make three more standard units (no picots). Turn the piece over again. Starting and ending with a standard unit, make seven more basic elements (eight bugles added). This piece has a total of 34 bugles.

[2] Leave the needle and thread on the spine edge and end and trim the remaining threads and tail.

[3] Make a second matching element.

Center double-S element

[1] Start a 5-yd. (4.6m) length of thread and make a basic element with 18 bugles.

[2] Turn the piece over and add the following units: standard, picot, two standard, *picot then standard* (repeat *–* five times), standard, picot, standard. You now have 35 bugles.

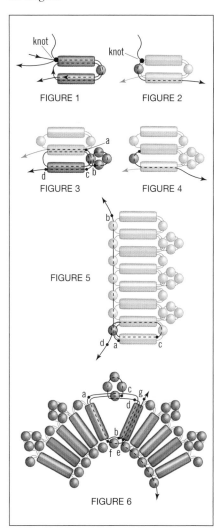

FIGURE 1   FIGURE 2

FIGURE 3   FIGURE 4

FIGURE 5

FIGURE 6

[a]

[b]

[c]

[d]

[e]

[3] Turn the piece again and add 17 more bugles, starting and ending with a standard unit. There are 52 bugles.
[4] Tie off both needles and glue the knots. Hide the picot-edge thread and cut off only this thread. Leave the starting tail and the spine needle and thread.

Assemble the necklace

Arrange the individual elements as they will appear on the finished necklace (**photo a**). Then join them as follows:

Circle to double S

[1] Thread a needle with 2 ft. (61cm) of single thread. Counting and starting on the left of the double S, attach the thread securely, and go through the spine beads until you come to the 17th bugle. Go down the bugle.
[2] Attach the eighth picot on the double S between any two picots of the circle as follows: Go through the bottom, left, and top beads of the eighth picot (**figure 7, point a**). Continue through the left-side bead of the right-hand (second) circle picot, the top of the standard unit between picots #2 and #1, and the right-side bead of picot #1. Continue through the top bead of the double S picot again (**a–b**) and tighten the thread.
[3] Go counterclockwise around circle picot #2 and out the top bead from right to left (**b–c**). Go left to right through the first spine bead on the double S center and circle through the picot and spine beads again (**c–d**).
[4] Go through the spine beads to attach circle picots #3–6 to spine beads #5 (**d–e**), 9, 13, and 17 (**photo b**).
[5] Finally, attach the eighth picot from the right-hand side of the double S between picots #6 and 7 on the circle. Go through the first standard unit bead, up the 17th bugle from the right, down the 16th, and around the left side of the eighth picot from the

right. Then make the attachment as in **figure 7** in reverse. End by going through the beads of the eighth picot and the 17th bugle from the right on the double S then all the spine beads except the last two from left to right. Tie off and hide the thread, seal the knots, and trim. Leave the starting tail in place.

Left-hand side S to double S

The side S elements are not symmetrical. One end has three picots and the other has five. Attach the last bugle on the three-picot end to the center double S between the top beads of picots #9 and 10, counting from the left (there are two standard units between these picots).
[1] Enter the right-hand side bead of picot #9 and go clockwise all the way around the picot and out the bottom bead toward the left (**figure 8, a–b**).
[2] Enter the bugle to the left of the picot and follow the thread path through the bugles and seeds to exit the top of the bugle to the left (**b–c**) of picot #10.
[3] Go left to right through the bottom bead of the picot and all the way around the picot. Exit the top bead of the picot from right to left (**c–d**).
[4] Then go through the bottom bugle of the left-hand S from right to left (**d–e**). Tie, bury, and trim.
[5] Pick up the needle on the left-hand edge of the double S. Counting from right to left on the side S, skip the seven spine beads on the three-picot end and the edge beads of the first two standard units. You will attach the edge bugle of the double S to the next two standard units of the side S behind the picot that is between them. Go through the standard unit edge bead to the right of the picot and continue through the bottom bead of the picot and the standard unit edge bead to the left of the picot (**photo c**).
[6] Go through the edge bugle from left to right, holding it behind the picot (**photo d**). Repeat the thread path, then end the thread securely and trim.

Basic elements to left-hand side S

Join one of the eight-bugle basic elements to the center section of the side S.

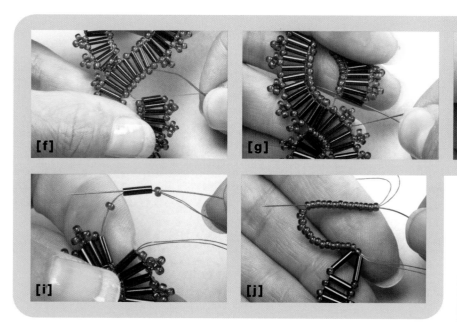

[f]

[g]

[h]

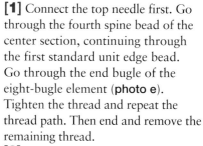

[i]

[j]

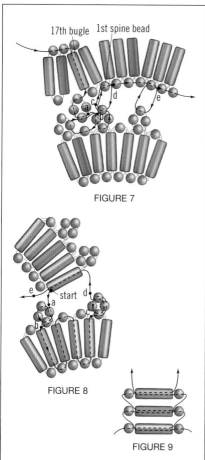

17th bugle   1st spine bead

FIGURE 7

FIGURE 8

e   start   d

FIGURE 9

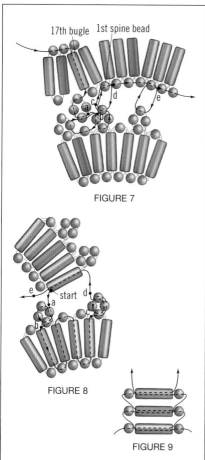

[1] Connect the top needle first. Go through the fourth spine bead of the center section, continuing through the first standard unit edge bead. Go through the end bugle of the eight-bugle element (**photo e**). Tighten the thread and repeat the thread path. Then end and remove the remaining thread.

[2] With the bottom needle, go through the fifth through first spine beads above the standard unit at the three-picot end. Coming out the first spine bead, go through the end bugle on the eight-bugle unit (**photo f**). Tighten the thread and repeat before ending it.

[3] To connect the ten-bugle element into the curve at the top of the S, take the bottom needle through the first standard unit, the base of the sixth picot, and the next standard unit. Then go through the bottom bugle, setting it behind the picot (**photo g**). Repeat the thread path.

[4] Using the same needle, go through the spine beads of the S element to the top. Then go through the spine beads of the ten-bugle element. End by going through the first spine bead in this section of the S element again (**photo h**).

[5] End and remove both threads.

[6] Repeat the joinings on the right-hand side of the necklace.

Make the strap

[1] Start a 4-yd. thread as for a basic element. With one needle, go through the last bugle of the ten-bugle element toward the outer edge. Take the other needle through the last bugle of the S element.

[2] Pick up an 11º, a bugle, and an 11º. With the other needle, go through the last 11º and the bugle (**photo i**).

[3] Following the directions for the basic element, make a standard, a picot, a standard, and a picot unit with the picots facing outward.

[4] With one needle, pick up an 11º and a bugle. Pick up an 11º on the other needle and pass it through the bugle in the opposite direction (**figure 9**) for the first ladder stitch. Continue in ladder stitch until the strap has a total of 17 bugles, including those in the basic element at the beginning.

[5] Make a standard unit. Resume ladder stitch until you have 30 bugles.

[6] Make a standard unit. Then alternate a ladder stitch and a standard unit until the strap has 38 bugles.

[7] To add the button, pick up three 11ºs on each needle. Cross both needles through the shank of the button and take each needle through the adjacent seed beads. Repeat the attachment as many times as possible. Weave back through the entire strap for strength and end the threads.

[8] Make the other strap like the first until you have 38 bugles.

[9] For the loop, pick up an 11º and a bugle on each needle. Pick up an 11º on one needle and cross the other needle through it. On one needle,

MATERIALS

- 15g 6mm Japanese bugle beads
- 10g size 11º seed beads
- small shank button for clasp
- Nymo B conditioned with beeswax or Fireline 6-lb. test
- 12 beading needles, #12 or 13
- G-S Hypo Cement

pick up enough 11ºs to make a loop that just fits over the button. Take the other needle through the loop of beads in the opposite direction (**photo j**). Work the needles back through the strap and end.

Beads & stones

Link a strand of stone beads to a bezeled or plain stone pendant

by **Louise Malcolm**

Hang a stone on a head pin and link it to a chain of beads on wrapped loops or make an open-back bezel of seed beads around a cabochon for the pendant. For the bezel, a band of right-angle weave is closed tightly around the top and bottom edges of the stone.

Making an oval bezel

If you use a thin cabochon like mine, only three rows of right-angle weave are needed for the bezel. (Thicker cabs require another row or two.)

[1] Start with 2 yd. (1.8m) of beading thread and make a base row of right-angle weave (Basics, p. 7) 35 stitches long or long enough to fit almost around the edge of the stone. The stitch you add to join the strip into a circle will make the fit perfect. Hold the strip around the stone edge to gauge fit (**photo a**).

[2] Join the strip into a circle: come out the last bead in the strip, pick up a bead, sew through the first bead in the strip (make sure the strip isn't twisted), pick up another seed bead, and sew back through the last bead of the strip.

[3] Come out the top bead on the joining stitch and make a second row of right-angle weave. Sew around the last stitch to exit the top

bead. Continue adding rows until the circle is wide enough to extend over the front and back of the stone by a few beads. End by exiting a top bead on the last row.

Inserting the cabochon

[1] To close the back of the bezel, narrow one end by going through two beads along the outside edge of the row. Then string one bead. Repeat around the end.

[2] On the front of the stone, go through two beads, pick up a bead, go through the next bead, and pick up a bead. Continue this pattern around the front of the bead, sewing through one bead on the sides of the stone, and two beads on the narrower ends (**photo b**).

[3] Test the fit of the cab in the bezel. The beadwork should overlap the back of the stone by about ⅛ in. (3mm). Go through all the beads on the edge again to tighten the edge. If necessary, you can tighten the edges again once the cab is in place.

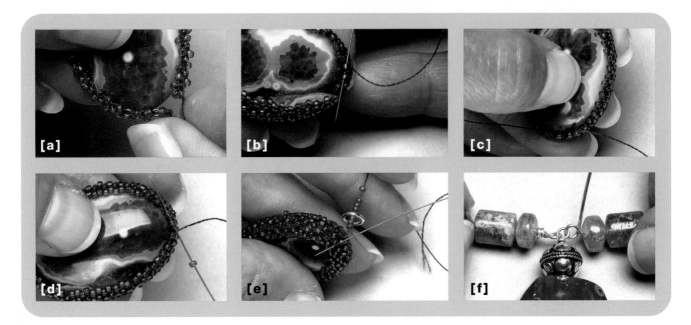

Weave through the beadwork until the needle exits the other edge.

[4] Insert the cab with the bottom against the finished lower edge and the narrow ends of the stone fitting into the tightly decreased sections of the bezel. Continue holding the piece as shown in **photo c** until you've tightened the beads around the top.

[5] To tighten the bezel around the top of the stone, sew through a seed bead, pick up a seed bead, and sew through the next bead, as in step 2. You may need to sew through two seed beads without picking up a bead to tighten the bezel. When you reach the narrow ends of the stone, pick up one seed bead and sew through two beads (**photo d**).

[6] Go through the edge beads two to three more times. If you notice unsightly gaps, string a thin bead into them. Weave the tail down into the side of the bezel, tying three or four half-hitch knots (Basics) between beads to keep the work very snug.

[7] Weave back to the bottom side and go through the edge beads two or three more times, pulling the thread tight. End with half-hitch knots.

[8] Finally, work the thread to the center top of the bezel and make a small loop of seed beads perpendicular to the face of the stone. String the 4mm ring on the loop (**photo e**). Go through the loop beads again. Then secure the thread and tail in the beadwork and cut the tails.

Making a bead dangle

String a 2–3mm silver bead, the stone bead, and a 4–6mm silver bead on the head pin. Make a wrapped loop (Basics) above the bead.

Making the necklace

For each bead or group of beads in the chain, use a piece of wire 3 in. (7.6cm) longer than the bead(s).

[1] Start at the center front of the necklace and prepare two stone beads to go on either side of the pendant. Make a wrapped loop on each piece of wire. String a bead or beads on each wire, and make the first half of wrapped loop on the other side. Pull the pendant loop or ring into both loops and complete the wraps (**photo f**).

[2] Continue making bead units by stringing a bead or collections of beads on a piece of wire and beginning a wrapped loop on either end. Link the bead units to each end of the necklace and complete the wraps. Continue until the necklace is within 1 in. (2.5cm) from the desired length, but do not complete the wraps on the final units.

[2] Pull one half of the clasp into the unwrapped loops on either end of the necklace. Check the fit and complete the wraps.

MATERIALS

strung necklace
- medium-large stone bead (jasper)
- 4–6mm silver bead
- 2–3mm silver bead
- 3-in. (7.6cm) head pin

bezeled cabochon
- stone cabochon, 30 x 20mm (ocean jasper)
- 2–3g seed beads, size 14º–15º
- Nymo B or Silamide beading thread
- 4mm silver soldered jump ring or split ring
- beading needles, #13

both necklaces
- 14–16-in. (36–41cm) strand 12–25mm stone beads or nuggets
- 1½ yd. (1.4m) 20- or 22-gauge sterling silver wire or colored wire
- clasp

Tools: chainnose pliers, roundnose pliers, wire cutters

Spiral rope chain

Gather glowing chips into a traditional spiral for an added twist

by **Linda Gettings**

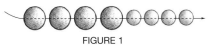

FIGURE 1

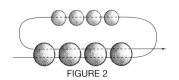

FIGURE 2

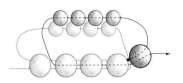

FIGURE 3

MATERIALS

- 30g size 11º seed beads
- 10g size 8º seed beads
- 16-in. (41cm) strand semi-precious stone chips
- Nymo B or D conditioned with beeswax
- beading needles, #10
- 2 bead tips
- clasp

Tools: chainnose pliers, roundnose pliers

Adding stone chips to a spiral rope gives it texture and color. It may look complicated, but this sophisticated necklace only uses one technique.

[1] Using an 8-ft. (2.4m) length of conditioned thread (Basics, p. 7) doubled, pick up four 8º and four 11º seed beads (**figure 1**). Leaving an 8-in. (20cm) tail, go through the 8ºs again in the same direction (**figure 2**).

[2] Pick up an 8º and four 11ºs. Skip the first 8º and sew through the other four 8ºs (**figure 3**). Keep the tension firm as you work. Repeat until you reach the desired length for this side.
[3] For the center section of the necklace, pick up an 8º and three stone chips. Continue making the spiral, substituting the chips for the 11ºs as shown in the photo above.
[4] Once the center section is the desired length, resume using 8ºs and 11ºs until this side of the necklace is the same length as the first.
[5] String a bead tip and an 11º on each end of the spiral rope. Go back through the tip, and secure the thread in the beadwork with a few half-hitch knots (Basics). Retrace the thread path to secure the bead tip, end the thread, and trim. Use chainnose pliers to close the bead tip over the 11º. Attach each clasp half to a bead tip with chainnose pliers.

Twining vines

Highlight an art bead with
lattice, vines, and flowers

by **Stacey Summerhill-Grady**

The inspiration for this necklace comes right from the backyard, where daisies and blue morning glories weave their way through the fence.

String the necklace base

[1] Cut a 36-in. (.9m) length of flexible beading wire. String a 6º seed bead and slide it to the center of the wire. Hold the cut ends together and string six 6ºs, sliding them against the first 6º strung. Now string the focal bead (**photo a**).

[2] Separate the wires and string 12 in. (30cm) of 6ºs on each wire. Tape the ends. If you plan to make this necklace large enough to fit over your head (no clasp), try it on and add beads if necessary.

Stitch the lattice

[1] Thread a needle with 2 yd. (1.8m) of conditioned Nymo or Fireline (Basics, p. 7). Anchor your thread with an overhand knot (Basics) between the fifth and sixth beads on either strand. Go through the beads toward the wire end, anchoring the thread with a half-hitch knot (Basics) after each bead. If the knots slide on the beading wire, dot them with glue. Bring your needle out the end bead (**photo b**).

[2] String four color A 11º seed beads and slide them against the 6ºs. Go through the first A again to form a circle around the beading wire (**photo c**).

[3] Pick up three As, a B, and three As. Skip the next A on the circle and go through the third A (**photo d**). String three As, a B, and three As and go through the first A of the circle (**photo e**). The circle now has two loops. Keep the tension snug.

[4] Go through the first three As and the B on the first loop to step down so you can begin the next row. Pick up three As, a B, and three As and go through the B on the second loop of row 1. String three As, a B, and three As and go through the B on the first row 1 loop (**photo f**). Pull the thread away from (not over) the lattice as you tighten each row. Step down through the first three As and the B on the first loop of the completed row. Continue adding rows until you reach the focal bead.

[5] Go through the Bs on the lattice's last row (**photo g**). Tighten the thread so the lattice closes around the beading wire next to the focal bead (**photo h**). Repeat to secure the beads.

[6] Then take the needle through the focal bead and the 6ºs below it. Start another section of lattice around the 6ºs below the focal bead, working toward the focal bead. End this small lattice section as before.

[7] Go back through the focal bead and cover the unfinished strand with lattice (steps 1–5) until it is the same length as the completed strand.

[8] If you plan to use a clasp to finish the ends, skip to "Add vines, leaves, and flowers." For a continuous loop necklace, string a crimp bead on either strand of beading wire and cross the other wire through it. Slide each wire through the first few 6ºs (**photo i**). Pull the wire tails to tighten all the beads and crimp the crimp bead (Basics). Trim the wire tails.

[9] Slide the crimp into the lattice to conceal it. Join the two sections of lattice with a few stitches. The join won't be an exact match of the lattice pattern, but you'll cover the seam with vines in the following steps.

Add vines, leaves, and flowers

The continuous loop necklace (no clasp) is finished when you complete step 6, below.

[1] Secure a 2-yd. length of thread in the beadwork at one of the unfinished

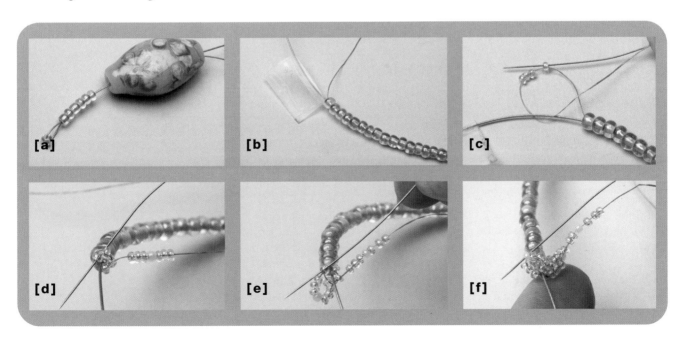

[a] [b] [c] [d] [e] [f]

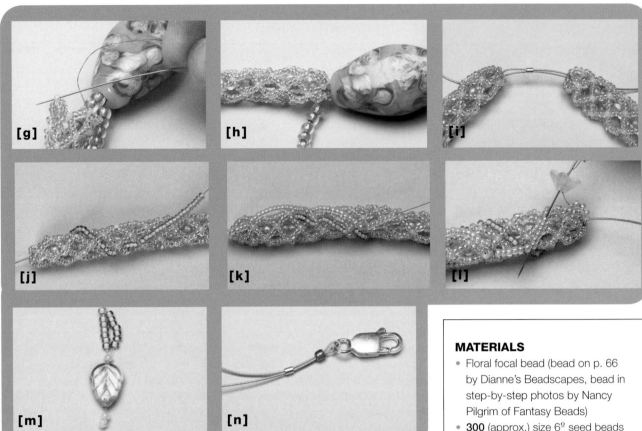

[g]

[h]

[i]

[j]

[k]

[l]

[m]

[n]

ends or at the focal bead. Using color C 11ºs, string about 6 in. (15cm) or more of beads and weave this strand loosely around and through the lattice (**photo j**). String another few inches of beads and repeat to the end of the lattice.

[2] Repeat step 1 with color D 11ºs (**photo k**).

[3] To add flowers and leaves to the vines, secure your thread in the beadwork at one of the unfinished ends (or at the focal bead for a continuous loop necklace). Sew through a few vine beads, pick up a flower or leaf, then sew back into the vine between the same two beads.

To string flowers, pick up a flower bead and an E 11º, skip the E, and go back through the flower to the vine (**photo l**).

To string a leaf, pick up two Es, a leaf bead, and an E. Skip the last E, and go back through the leaf and two Es to the vine. Decorate one vine at a time.

[4] Start a new thread in the lattice below the focal bead and work a short vine around this section. Then string another 1½–2 in. (3.8–5cm) of Cs or Ds to form a strand of fringe. Add a decorative finish to each fringe by stringing a C, a leaf, and two Cs. Turn, skip the end C, and go back through the newly added beads. String seven Cs or Ds and go up through the eighth bead on the fringe (**photo m**). Continue through the vine beads until you reach the focal bead. Repeat, making several strands of fringe below the focal bead. (These fringes are half the total number.)

[5] Repeat step 4, using D 11ºs.

[6] When you've completed the fringe, add a few flowers to the vines below the focal bead, secure the thread, and trim.

Attach the clasp

[1] To finish the necklace ends with a clasp, string a crimp bead and an 8º on the beading wire. Take the wire through the loop on one of the clasp parts and back through the 8º and crimp bead (**photo n**). Slide the tail through a few 6ºs along the core and tighten the wire to form a small loop around the clasp.

[2] Crimp the crimp bead and trim the excess wire.

[3] Repeat at the other end.

MATERIALS

- Floral focal bead (bead on p. 66 by Dianne's Beadscapes, bead in step-by-step photos by Nancy Pilgrim of Fantasy Beads)
- **300** (approx.) size 6º seed beads or 3mm round pressed-glass beads
- size 11º seed beads
  40g (for lattice), color A
  20g (for lattice), color B
  20g (for vines), color C
  20g (for vines), color D
  3g (for leaf and flower highlights), gold color E
- **2** size 8º seed beads
- **30** (approx.) Czech leaves, with a vertical hole
- **25** (approx.) Czech glass flowers
- crimp bead or **2** crimp beads and clasp
- Nymo D conditioned with beeswax or Fireline 6 lb. test
- beading needles, #12
- flexible beading wire, .019
- G-S Hypo Cement

Tools: crimping pliers

Zigzag necklace

Use simple picots to form a lacy chain

by **Pat Duerfeldt**

This quick, easy necklace looks great with casual styles. Use one type of seed bead for a simple, lacy accent, or experiment with using multiple colors or different bead sizes.

[1] Measure your neck to determine the finished length of the choker.

[2] Measure a length of thread approximately four times longer than the desired length of your finished necklace. Slide a needle to the center of the thread and tie the ends around the clasp with a surgeon's knot (Basics, p. 7). You'll use the thread doubled.

[3] Pick up five beads and slide them against the clasp, covering the thread tails at the knot (**photo a**). Sew through the third and fourth beads from the clasp in the same direction as before (**photo b**). Pull

the thread tight. This creates a three-bead picot.

[4] Pick up two beads and slide them toward the clasp. Sew back through the fifth and sixth beads. Pull tight. Continue picking up two beads and looping back through the last bead of the previous group and the first bead of the newly added group to make picots.

[5] To finish the necklace, string two beads and the other clasp half. Go through the clasp and back through the last two seed beads. Sew through the three beads that make the last picot and up through the last two

seed beads and clasp once more (**photo c**). Sew back through the beadwork, tying two or three half-hitch knots between beads. Glue the knots and trim the tails.

MATERIALS

- 15g seed beads, size 8º
- Nymo D bead thread
- beeswax or Thread Heaven
- beading needles, #10
- clasp
- G-S Hypo Cement

[a] [b] [c]

Seaside stitching

Fringe a necklace with
faceted seed beads and freshwater pearls

by **Lisa Olson Tune**

Seashore finds and a stitch adaptation
inspired this kelplike necklace embedded
with pearls. Use tiny seed beads for the
fringe, which branches out like an exotic
marine plant. The finished necklace
looks luxurious, yet seed beads keep
the materials cost low.

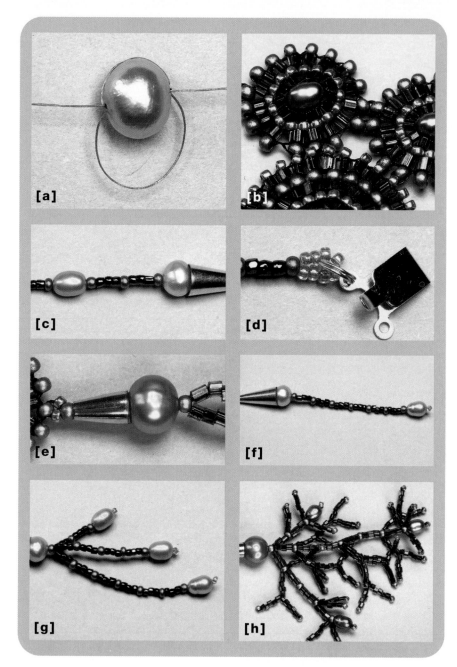

[a]

[b]

[c]

[d]

[e]

[f]

[g]

[h]

Sides

[1] Select four points at the outer edges of the center design to anchor the sides to the circles. Secure a single thread in the circles and come out at one of the anchor points. String a gold 14º, an 11º, a cone (narrow end first), a potato pearl, and an 11º.

[2] String 26 groups of three 12ºs and an 11º, intermittently substituting one rice pearl for three 12ºs (**photo c**).

[3] String eight gold 14ºs and a split ring attached to a clasp's loop. Go back through all the beads strung in step 1 and 2, tightening the thread to close the loop of 14ºs (**photo d**). After going through the 14º adjacent to the circle, sew through the nearest gold 14º on the circle's edge.

[4] To start the second strand (**photo e**), string a gold 14º, then go through the 11º, the cone, the potato pearl, and the 11º strung in step 1.

[5] Repeat step 2. Go through the loop around the clasp, then back through the second strand to the circle's anchor seed. Weave the tail into the circle and trim.

[6] Repeat steps 1–5, making a total of four double-strand sides.

Dangles

[1] Select three points along the bottom edge of the central circles to anchor drops (see photo, p. 71). Weave a single thread into a circle and come out at one of the anchor points. String a gold 14º, an 11º, a cone, a potato pearl, and an 11º.

[2] Add six groups of three 12ºs and one 11º, then string a rice pearl and a gold 14º. Skip the 14º, and go back through the other beads, the cone, and the 11º (**photo f**).

[3] Add a gold 14º, then go through the circle's anchor seed, the 11º, the cone, the pearl, and the 11º.

[4] Repeat step 2, but string four groups of seed beads, not six. Go back through the gold 14º, the anchor seed, the 14º, the cone, the pearl, and the 11º.

[5] Repeat step 4, but string two groups of seed beads (**photo g**). Weave in the tail securely and cut. Repeat, making three dangles in total.

Beaded circles

[1] String a potato pearl on a single strand of conditioned Nymo B (Basics, p. 7) and make a surgeon's knot (Basics), leaving a 15-in. (38cm) tail. Pull the knot into the pearl's hole. Go through the pearl again to encircle it with thread (**photo a**).

[2] Pick up two brown 14º seed beads. Work in brick stitch (Basics and **figure 1**) around the pearl, anchoring the stitches to the base thread.

[3] Work the next five rows as follows, increasing (**figure 2**) as necessary to keep the circles flat: row 2, gold 14ºs; row 3, 12ºs; row 4, 11ºs; and row 5, 12ºs.

[4] On the sixth row, pick up a gold 14º and go under the thread bridge (**figure 3**). Repeat around the edge. Weave in both tails securely, then trim. Repeat, making a total of seven beaded circles.

[5] Make six smaller circles using rice pearls. Work four rows: brown 14ºs, gold 14ºs, 12ºs, and an edge of gold 14ºs.

[6] Arrange the circles as shown in the necklace on p. 71 or plan a design of your own. Attach the circles securely with square knots (Basics and **photo b**). Weave in the tails and trim.

FIGURE 1

FIGURE 2

FIGURE 3

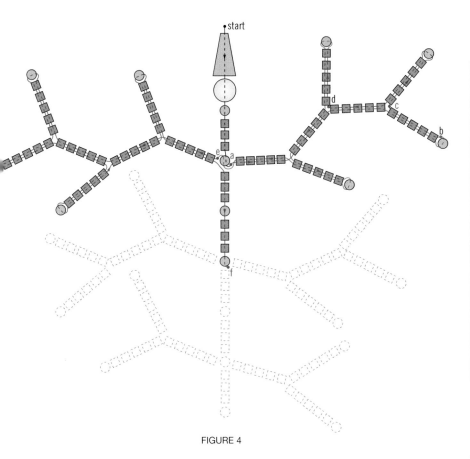

FIGURE 4

MATERIALS

necklace 19 in. (48cm)

- **14** 8–10mm potato-shaped freshwater pearls
- **43** 4 x 7mm rice-shaped freshwater pearls
- 15g size 12º 2-cut seed beads, brown
- 5g size 14º 2-cut seed beads, brown
- 5g size 14º seed beads, gold
- 10g size 11º seed beads, gold
- **7** ¼-in. (6mm) cones
- **4** 4–5mm split rings
- two-strand clasp
- Nymo B and O, black, conditioned with Thread Heaven
- beading needles, #12

Editor's note: To change the length of this 19-in. (48cm) necklace, adjust the number of beads on each side strand.

If you can't find 12ºs and 14ºs, you can substitute 11ºs and 15ºs.

Fringe

Make the side fringe shorter as it approaches the clasp.

[1] Using Nymo O, weave a single thread into a circle near a side strand. Go through the strand's gold 14º, 11º, cone, pearl, and five seed beads.

[2] String 20 brown 14ºs and a gold 14º (**figure 4, a–b**). Turn, skip the gold 14º, and go back through five beads (**b–c**).

[3] Pick up five brown 14ºs and a gold 14º. Turn, skip the gold 14º, and go back through ten brown 14ºs (**c–d**).

[4] Repeat step 3 twice and go through the highlighted 11º (**d–e**).

[5] Repeat step 2–4, but skip the 11º and go through the next eight beads (**e–f**).

[6] Repeat steps 2–5 twice, making a total of three pairs of branched fringe. (Not shown in figure 4.)

[7] Continue along the strand as before and make three more pairs of branched fringe, but use 15 brown 14ºs instead of 20. Then make three more pairs, using ten brown 14ºs (**figure 4**, outlined area).

[8] Use the same technique to add fringe to the drops (**photo h**).

Entrapped donut

Two-drop peyote brings stones and pearls together

by **Janet-Beth McCann Flynn**

Shape and texture are compelling aspects of stone donuts. This necklace combines a group of small donuts with different size holes and a large centerpiece donut with two-drop peyote stitch, which works up quickly. The center is trimmed with small teardrop pearls, and closes almost invisibly with a snap.

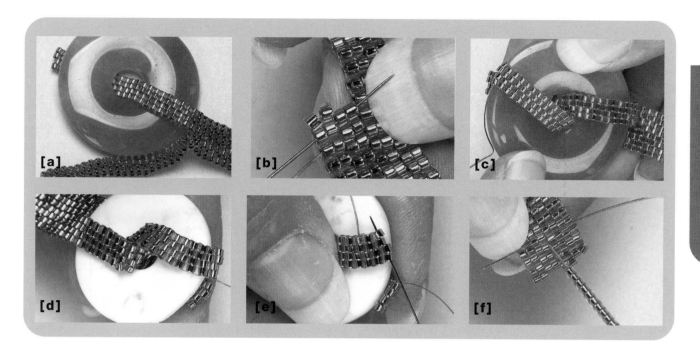

[a] [b] [c]

[d] [e] [f]

Peyote strips

[1] Using a long, comfortable length of doubled thread, position a stop bead (Basics, p. 7) about 4 in. (10cm) from the end. (If using Fireline, don't double it.)

[2] Pick up ten cylinder beads, skip the last four beads, and go through the next two (figure 1, a–b). Pick up two beads, skip the next two, and go through the last two (b–c).

[3] Continue working two-drop peyote (Basics and c–d) until the strip is 1½ in. (3.8cm) long.

[4] Make one peyote stitch half the width of the strip (figure 2, a–b). Turn and add two beads for the next row (b–c). Continue stitching four-bead rows until the strip is long enough to span the diameter of the large donut, passing through the donut's hole, as shown in photo a.

[5] Start a new length of thread and secure it in the wide strip a few rows before the narrow four-bead strip. End by sewing through the four beads next to the narrow strip (photo b). Work a second narrow, four-bead strip until it's the same length as the first. Secure the thread in the beadwork and trim.

[6] Weave one narrow strip over the donut, through the hole, and under the other side of the donut (photo a). Position the other narrow strip under the donut, through the hole, and over the other side of the donut (photo c).

[7] Using the remaining thread on the first narrow strip, join the two strips by sewing through the four beads on the second narrow strip (figure 3, a–b). Then work two-drop peyote across all eight beads (b–c) for 1½ in.

[8] Repeat steps 4–7 with one of the small donuts. To fit both narrow strips through the donut's hole, fold the first strip against the side of the hole and pull the other strip through to the front on the other side of the hole. The strips will form a tuck on the back (photo d). You may need to add a few extra rows of peyote to each strip so they reach the edge of the donut. Then join the strips (photo e) and stitch an eight-bead strip 1½ in. long, as in step 7.

[9] Repeat step 8 with the second small donut. Then work two-drop peyote over the full width of the strip until this side of the necklace is long enough to reach ½ in. (1.3cm) past the center of the back of your neck.

[10] Remove the stop bead from the other end of the strip, secure it in the beadwork, and trim.

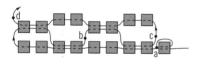

FIGURE 1

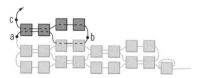

FIGURE 2

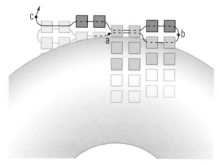

FIGURE 3

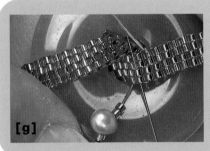

[g]

[h]

[11] Start a new thread, weave it into the tail end of the peyote strip, and repeat steps 8 and 9 for the second side of the necklace.

[12] For the closure, sew a shank button or a flat bead to the top of the peyote strip ½ in. from one end of the necklace. On the other end of the necklace, pick up enough beads to make a loop that will fit over the button. Position the loop the same distance from the edge as the button (photo f). Reinforce both.

Pearl embellishment

[1] Secure a new thread in a narrow peyote strip at the center of the large donut at the front of the necklace. Exit two edge beads and string two cylinder beads, a pearl, and two cylinders. Sew through the next two edge beads (photo g), then sew through the next two beads so the thread exits at the edge of the strip.

[2] Repeat step 1 until you've reached the end of the narrow strip. Then repeat on the other edge (photo h).

[3] Repeat steps 1 and 2 on the remaining narrow strip at the center of the large donut.

MATERIALS

- 38–40mm stone donut with a center hole 12mm or larger
- 4 18–20mm stone donuts with center holes 6mm or larger
- 8 in. (20cm) 4–5mm pearls, top drilled
- ½-in. (1.3cm) shank button or flat bead for clasp
- 20g Japanese cylinder beads
- Nymo B or D conditioned with beeswax, Silamide, or Fireline 8–12 lb. test
- beading needles, #12 or 13

Victorian lace choker

Combine brick stitch, peyote, and netting for a delicate choker

by **Lisa Norris**

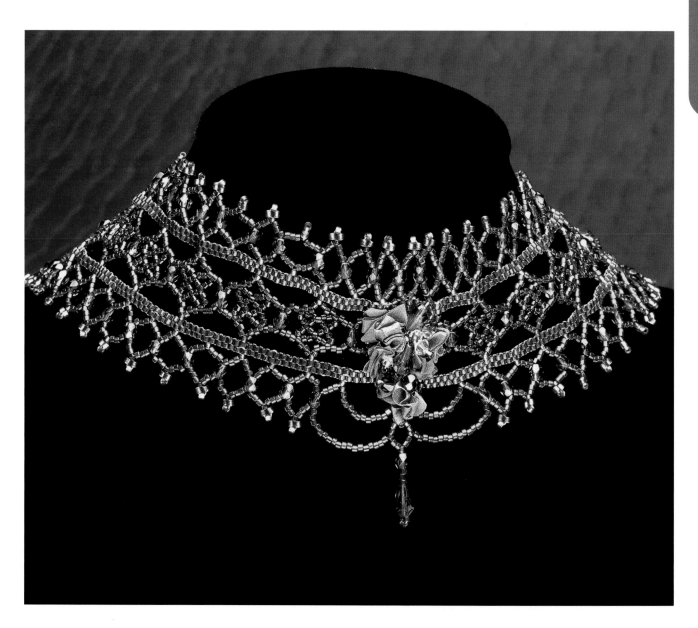

Lace motifs are joined with peyote stitch bands for a necklace that is decorated with ribbon embroidery, pearls, small buttons, small beads, and crystals. You can also substitute a fancy button for the centerpiece.

[a]

[b]

[c]

Ribbon embroidery centerpiece

Refer to **figure 1** as you work the following steps.

[1] Using a 1-yd. (.9m) length of thread, leave a 12-in. (30cm) tail, and work a two-bead ladder (Basics, p. 7) 11 stacks long with color A cylinder beads.

[2] Work the next seven rows in brick stitch (Basics), adding a stack of two beads per stitch and decreasing each row by one stack. Then turn the piece, thread a needle on the tail, and work the four rows above the ladder.

[3] To make a ribbon flower, cut a 1-in. (2.5cm) length of ¼-in. (6mm) wide silk ribbon for each flower. Using a sharps needle and 1 yd. of thread, weave into the brick-stitch centerpiece, and exit a bead where you want the first flower. Sew a straight line of medium-length stitches along the center of a ribbon piece. Gather the stitches and sew back into the same bead the thread exits (**photo a**) to complete the first flower. Make as many flowers as desired using the same thread.

[4] Sew small pearls, crystals, and bead or button accents between the flowers to fill the front of the centerpiece. Then end the thread by weaving it into the beadwork and trim.

Bead-lace bands

Individual lace medallions are connected between two peyote bands with netting. A row of picots trims the outer edges.

Peyote strips

[1] Determine the length of the peyote strips. Measure your neck where you want the choker to lie. Subtract the width of the centerpiece and ¾ in. (2cm) for the length of the

MATERIALS

- **5–10** assorted small pearls, crystals, beads, and buttons
- **85** or more 4mm Czech fire-polished glass beads
- Japanese cylinder beads
  20g color A
  7.5g color B
- 7mm teardrop with vertical hole
- shank button for clasp
- Nymo D conditioned with beeswax, to match beads and silk ribbons
- beading needles, #10–12
- sharps needles, #12 (for centerpiece)
- 1 yd. (.9m) ¼-in. (6mm) wide silk ribbon

clasp. Divide the remaining length in half.

[2] Working with a comfortable length of thread, pick up three As (**figure 2, a–b**). Go back through the first A (**b–c**). Pick up an A and go through the third A (**c–d**). Pick up an A and go through the next-to-last A added (**d–e**). Continue working even-count peyote (Basics) until you reach the length determined in step 1.

[3] Make a second strip as in step 1. Then make two more strips 12 rows longer (six beads along each edge).

[4] Position the first peyote strip so the edge-up bead nestles against the edge bead on the next-to-last row of the brick-stitch centerpiece as in **figure 1**. The down bead will fit against the top bead on the row below. Stitch the two pieces together as shown (**figure 3, a–c** and **photo b**). End the thread in the brick-stich centerpiece.

[5] Stitch the other short peyote strip to the opposite side of the brick stitch centerpiece. Then stitch the two longer, bottom strips to the brick-stitch centerpiece.

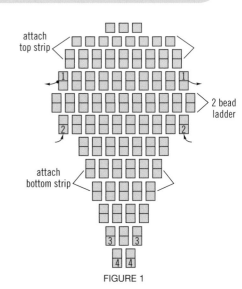

FIGURE 1

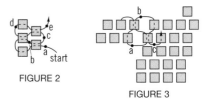

FIGURE 2

FIGURE 3

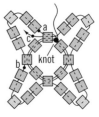

FIGURE 4

Lace medallions

You make each medallion separately, but you can work them in a series on a long length of thread. Start with 6–8 ft. (1.8–2.4m). The 11-in. (28cm) lace portion of this necklace has 16 medallions.

[1] To make the first medallion, pick up eight color B beads to 6 in. (15cm) from the tail. Tie the beads into a tight circle with a surgeon's knot (Basics) and go through the beads again. Continue through the first bead.

[2] Pick up two Bs, an A, and two Bs. Skip one bead on the circle and go

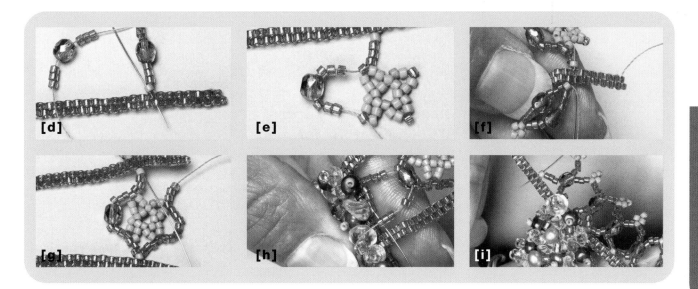

through the next bead (**figure 4, a–b**). Repeat three more times, then end by going through the first bead on the circle again (**b–c**). End the thread in the beadwork with a few half hitches (Basics). Go through a few beads and trim the threads. Make as many medallions as the starting thread will allow.

Join strips and medallions

[1] There are a number of ways to join the medallions between the two peyote strips, but here's how it is done on the purple necklace: Anchor a 2-yd. (1.8m) length of beading thread in the end of a top peyote strip, exiting the seventh bead on the top of the strip (**figure 5, point a**). (If your peyote strips don't work out with the same multiple as mine, adjust the connection points as needed to space the medallions evenly.)

[2] To make the first picot motif above the lace band, pick up a B, three As, a 4mm bead, three As, and four Bs. Go back through the first of the four Bs toward the start (**photo c** and **figure 5, a–b**) to make a three-bead picot.

[3] Pick up three As, a 4mm, and three As. Go back through the first B strung and into the eighth bead on the top of the peyote strip (**b–c**). Exit the bottom edge bead on the top of the strip, between the seventh and eighth beads (**photo d**).

[4] Pick up a B and three As and go through the A at the center of a loop on the medallion (**c–d**). Pick up three As, a 4mm bead, and three As. Go

through the A on the next loop of the medallion (**photo e**).

[5] Pick up three As and a B and go through the eighth bead from the end on the inner edge of the bottom peyote strip. Continue through the outer-edge bead between the seventh and eighth beads on the inner edge.

[6] Pick up a B, three As, a 4mm, three As, and four Bs. Make a picot as in **photo c** and pick up three As, a 4mm, and three As. Go back through the B below the peyote strip and through the next bead toward the end of the strip. Continue through the seventh bead from the end of the inner edge and go through the B (**photo f and e–f**).

[7] Pick up three As, and go through the A on the next loop of the medallion. For the outer edge of the edge medallions only, pick up seven As (the bead marked with an X in **figure 5** will be replaced by the 4mm bead you picked up between the first and second medallion loops on subsequent connections). Go through the A on the last loop of the medallion. Pick up three As and go through the B below the top peyote strip and the eighth bead on the bottom of the strip (**photo g and f–g**).

[8] Zigzag through the top strip to exit the fourth bead from the previous picot motif (**g–h**). Make another picot motif, attaching the first side to the crystal on the adjacent edge of the first picot (**h–i**). Zigzag through the strip to exit the fourth bead from the

picot motif (**i–j**). Make a picot motif in the same manner (**j–k**).

[9] Sew through the side of the next medallion and go through the tenth bead on the bottom strip from the first medallion (**k–l**). Make a picot motif and zigzag back through the strip toward the first medallion, exiting the bottom of the strip four beads from the picot motif (**l–m**). Make a picot motif, connecting each side to the 4mm beads on the adjacent motifs (**m–n**). Then zigzag back through the strip to the second medallion (**n–o**) and connect it to the first medallion (**o–p**).

[10] Continue connecting medallions and making picot motifs until you have connected the last medallion on the first side of the centerpiece and made one more picot motif along the top.

[11] Zigzag through the top strip to the side of the centerpiece. Work down the side and exit the bead marked **1** on **figure 1**. Pick up three to four As and go through the 4mm bead on the near edge of the last medallion. Pick up four to five As and go up into the centerpiece through the bead marked **2** (**photo h**). Work up through the centerpiece to exit the fourth bead past the last top picot motif.

[12] Work the next three top picot motifs evenly spaced above the centerpiece (**photo i**).

[13] Work down the other side of the centerpiece to exit the other **1** bead. Pick up three to four As, a 4mm, and four to five As and enter the

centerpiece through the B bead. Go back up the centerpiece to the top strip and space the next two top picot motifs as in **figure 5**.

[14] Work the other side of the necklace in the mirror image of the first.

Center bottom swag

[1] Secure a new thread in the bottom peyote strip and exit the fourth bead from the picot motif next to the centerpiece. Pick up a B, 12 As, a B, and enter the **3** bead on the centerpiece. Sew through the centerpiece as shown, and exit the other **3** bead. Pick up a B, 12 As, and a B. Sew through the fourth bead from the picot motif on the other side of the centerpiece and the two edge beads above (**figure 6, a–b**).

[2] Sew through the bottom edge bead to exit the next bead on the strip. Go through the last B. Pick up three As, and go through the 4mm on the picot motif. Pick up 20 As and a B. Go up through the **4** bead on the centerpiece and down the other **4** bead (**c–d**).

[3] Pick up a B and 20 As and go through the 4mm on the picot on the other side. Pick up three As and go through the first B strung for the swag and the next bead on the bottom edge of the strip (**d–e**).

[4] Zigzag through the strip and the centerpiece to a **4** bead, then sew through the B and two As (**e–f**).

[5] Pick up two As, a B, a 4mm, three As, a teardrop, an A, a B, and an A. Go back up the teardrop, three As, the 4mm bead, and a B. Pick up two As and sew through the two As and the B below the other **4** bead (**f–g**). End the thread in the centerpiece.

Clasp

[1] Secure a new 1-yd. length of thread in the top peyote strip near the end picot motif. Weave through the picot motif and exit the 4mm bead on the outer edge. Pick up three As and a B, and sew through the third-to-last beads below on the peyote strip (**figure 7, a–b**).

[2] Pick up six As and go through the X bead on the outside of the first

medallion. Pick up six As and sew through the third-to-last beads on the bottom strip (**b–c**).

[3] Sew up through the next-to-last beads on the strip (**c–d**) and the last bead strung. Work peyote stitch, adding five beads as shown (**d–e**).

[4] Work three more rows of peyote stitch (**e–h**).

[5] Zigzag back through the last row of peyote (**h–i**). Pick up an even number of beads to make a loop that will fit around the button clasp. Sew through the next single up bead on the last peyote row (**i–j**). Work a row of peyote stitch around the loop of beads.

[6] Weave down the peyote edge and exit the third bottom edge bead on the bottom strip. Pick up a B and three As, and sew through the 4mm bead on the edge of the picot below. Follow the thread path through the picot and end the thread in the peyote strip.

[7] Repeat steps 2–4 on the other end of the necklace. Then sew the button on the center of the band.

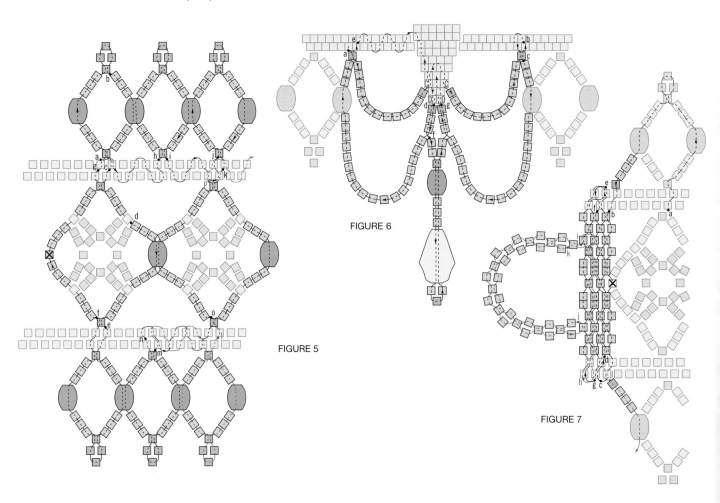

FIGURE 6

FIGURE 5

FIGURE 7

WIREWORK

A chain of pearls

Space lustrous pearls on chain for an easy, elegant necklace

by **Irina Miech**

This necklace exemplifies the theory that less is more. If you use high-quality beads in a simple design that doesn't get in the way of the materials, the beads are able to take center stage, so a little goes a long way.

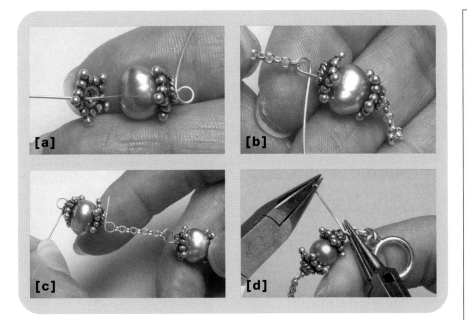

[a]

[b]

[c]

[d]

The necklace on the right on p. 82 is made with three links of drawn cable chain between each of five pearls capped at both ends with a silver bead cap. The drawn cable chain features fine, elongated links that are almost invisible between the substantial potato pearls. The other necklace version shown uses five-link segments of a wide, round rollo chain between the pearl units.

Rollo chain necklace

[1] Cut the wire into lengths 2 in. (5cm) longer than a pearl and two bead caps.

[2] Make the first half of a wrapped loop (Basics, p. 7) an inch from the end of the wire.

[3] Slide a bead cap, convex side toward the loop, a pearl, and a bead cap on the wire (**photo a**).

[4] Begin a second wrapped loop in the same plane as the first, leaving a small space for wrapping between the bead caps and the loops.

[5] Cut two nine-link pieces of rollo chain.

[6] Slide the end link of a piece of chain onto each loop (**photo b**). Complete the wraps (Basics).

[7] Make two more pearl units and link one to each chain end (**photo c**).

[8] Repeat steps 5–7 until the necklace is the desired length, minus the length of the clasp. Then attach the loops of the clasp to the loops on the end pearl units (**photo d**).

Five-pearl necklace

[1] Cut a piece of wire ¾ in. (1.9cm) longer than a pearl and two bead caps. Make a plain loop (Basics) at one end.

[2] Slide a bead cap, a pearl, and a bead cap on the wire. Make a second loop in the same plane as the first. Make five pearl units.

[3] Cut four three-link pieces of drawn cable chain.

[4] Open a loop (Basics) on a pearl unit and connect it to an end link on a piece of chain from step 3. Close the loop (Basics).

[5] Continue linking the chain pieces with pearl units.

[6] Repeat steps 5–7 until you have five pearls linked with chain. Divide the remaining desired length of the necklace minus the length of the clasp in half, cut two pieces of chain that length, and link them to the end pearls. Attach the clasp to the ends of the chain with split rings.

MATERIALS
both projects
- 4 ft. (1.2m) 22-gauge sterling silver wire, half hard
- clasp

rollo chain necklace
- **12–15** 6–8mm potato pearls
- **24–30** 6–8mm sterling silver bead caps
- **24–30** 2–3mm round sterling silver beads (optional)
- 10–14 in. (26–36cm) sterling silver 2.2mm rollo chain

five-pearl necklace
- **5** 6–8mm potato pearls
- **10** 6–8mm sterling silver bead caps
- **10** 2–3mm round sterling silver beads (optional)
- 10–14 in. (26–36cm) sterling silver 6.6mm drawn cable
- **2** 5mm split rings (5-pearl version)

Tools: chainnose pliers, roundnose pliers, wire cutters

Editor's note: If the bead caps have large holes, you may need to place a 2mm or 3mm round silver bead between the bead caps and the loops.

An elegant use for leftover chain

Create a fun and sophisticated necklace with beads and chain

by **Irina Miech**

After you've been making jewelry for a while, you may find yourself with lots of 3–4-in. (7.6–10cm) lengths of chain. They're too good to throw away, but what will you ever do with them? This necklace answers that question beautifully and, in addition, solves the problem of what to do with all those leftover beads you've been accumulating.

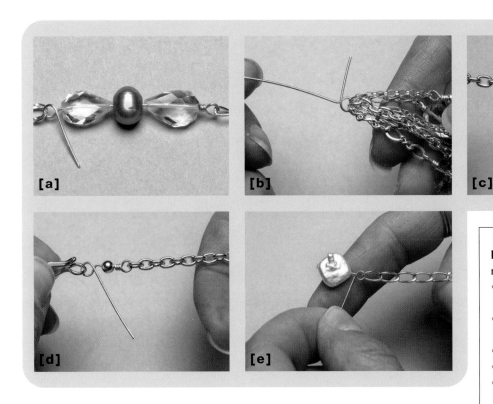

MATERIALS

necklace 16 in. (41cm)

- **23** or more pearls, crystals, or stones
- **4** 4mm sterling silver beads or crystals
- **2** cones
- lobster claw or hook clasp
- 1½–2 yd. (1.4–1.8m) 22-gauge sterling silver wire, half hard
- 66 in. (1.7m) or more silver chains of different sizes and shapes
- 1–2 in. (2.5–5cm) chain with links large enough to accommodate clasp
- **2** in. (5cm) head pin

Tools: chainnose pliers, roundnose pliers, wire cutters

[1] To make a beading unit, cut a piece of wire 2–3 in. (5–7.6cm) longer than the bead(s). Start a wrapped loop (Basics, p.7) about 1½ in. (3.8cm) from one end of the wire. Slide the end link of a piece of chain into the loop, then finish the wraps. String the bead(s) on the wire and begin another wrapped loop. Slide the end of another chain section into the loop (**photo a**). Complete the wraps.

[2] Assemble six strands of chain and bead units as described in step 1. Each strand should be about 10 in. (25cm) long, plus or minus ¼ in. (6mm).

[3] Cut a 4-in. (10cm) piece of wire and begin a large wrapped loop that will fit inside a cone. Working on one end of the necklace, slide the end link of each chain strand onto the loop (**photo b**) and complete the wraps.

[4] Slide the cone on the wire and over the loop and ends of chain. Pick up a 4mm bead or crystal on the wire and begin a wrapped loop. Slide the end link of a 2–3 in. piece of chain onto the loop (**photo c**), finish the wraps, and trim the excess wire.

[5] Repeat steps 3 and 4 on the other end of the necklace.

[6] To attach the clasp, cut a 2–3 in. piece of wire and start a wrapped loop. Slide the end link on one end of the necklace onto the loop and complete the wraps. Connect the loop to the loop on the clasp (**photo d**). Complete the wraps.

[7] Connect a 1–2 in. (2.5–5cm) piece of large link chain (that will accommodate the clasp) to the other end of the necklace with a 4mm bead unit as in step 6.

[8] To finish, string a small bead on the head pin and begin a wrapped loop above it. Attach this loop to the end of the large-link chain (**photo e**) and complete the wraps.

Radiant color

Sparkling crystals highlight jewel-toned dichroic spacers

by **Irina Miech**

These beautiful, two-hole, dichroic glass spacer beads by Ron McGuire flash and sparkle when paired with crystals. You can use crystals in a multitude of hues to highlight the brilliant hues and tones of the spacers.

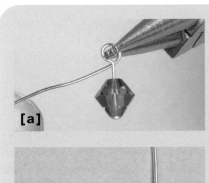

[a]

[b]

[c]

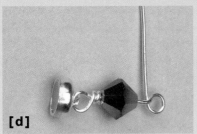

[d]

[e]

Editor's note: A magnetic clasp is used in the step-by-step photos shown here. The magnetic clasp works well for a bracelet, but we recommend using an S-hook or toggle clasp for the necklace for better security.

[1] Put two crystals aside for the clasp. String 280 crystals on head pins and make the first half of a wrapped loop close to each crystal (Basics, p. 7 and **photo a**). Attach four crystals to each chain link, two crystals per side. Cut the chain into ten three-link segments and ten four-link segments (**photo b**).

[2] Cut 22 3-in. pieces of wire. Make the first half of a wrapped loop at one end of each wire.

[3] To assemble the necklace, string a wire through one hole in a spacer bead and make the first half of a wrapped loop on the other side. Keep the loop close to the spacer. Attach the end link of a three-link chain section to this loop and finish the wraps (**photo c**). Repeat with a second wire going through the spacer's second hole and a four-link component.

[4] Attach the loop on a third piece of wire to the available end link on the three-link segment from step 3. Complete the wraps. Thread the wire through another spacer and make the first half of a wrapped loop as before. Connect a three-link segment and complete the wraps. Repeat with the second hole, connecting a four-link segment. Continue connecting spacers with three-link segments on the inner holes and four-link segments on the outer holes. Don't connect the chains to the last loops on the end spacers.

[5] Cut two more 3-in. pieces of wire. Make half a wrapped loop on one end of each wire and thread each clasp half onto a loop. Finish the wraps. String a crystal reserved in step 1 onto the wire and make the first half of another wrapped loop (**photo d**). Repeat with the other clasp half.

[6] Try on the necklace to determine how many links to add between the end spacer and the clasp assembly (or whether to add another spacer for a better fit). Cut four chain segments with the required number of links. Embellish with crystals as before.

[7] Attach each chain segment to an unfinished loop on the end spacers and finish the wraps. Slide the unfinished loop on one clasp assembly onto the end links of both segments on one end of the necklace (**photo e**). Finish the loop. Repeat on the other end of the necklace.

MATERIALS

necklace 18 in. (46cm)

- **340–360** 6mm bicone crystals
- **11–12** 2-hole glass spacer beads, 1 or 2 colors
- **340–360** 24-gauge (fine) sterling silver head pins
- **6–7 ft.** (1.8-2.1m) 22-gauge sterling silver wire, half hard
- **40 in.** (1m) sterling silver curb chain (5 links per inch/2.5cm)
- S-hook or toggle clasp

Tools: roundnose pliers, chainnose pliers, wire cutters

Editor's note: You can make a matching bracelet usinging the same technique. Simply shorten the length to fit your wrist and use three-link components on both sides of the bracelet.

Embellished raku

by **Wendy Witchner**

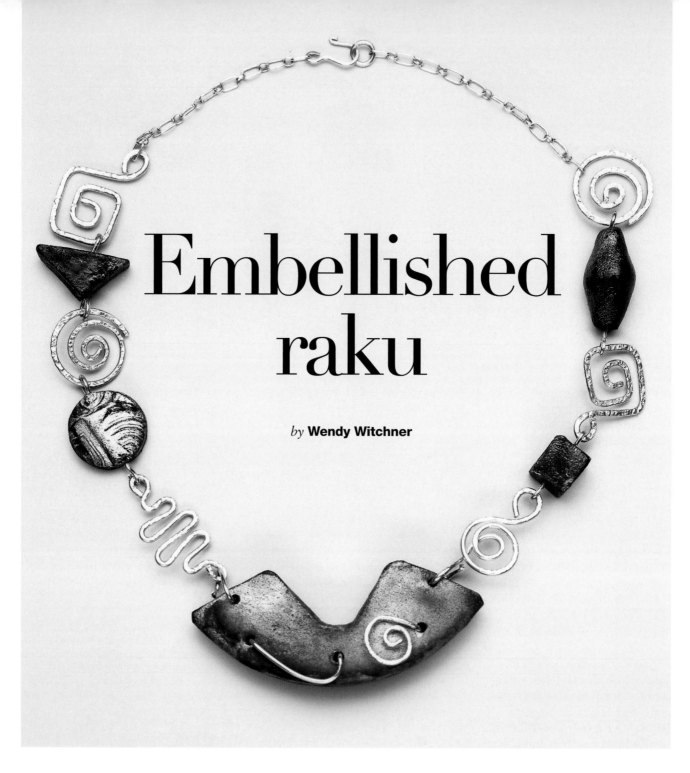

Link a diverse mix of beads with wire

To integrate the large centerpiece bead, stitch through it, using wire as both a connector and a design element.

[1] Using 16-gauge wire, make the decorative connectors shown in the templates in **figure 1**. This necklace uses two As, two Bs, one C, and one D. (You can vary the combinations as you'd like, but you'll need one with a long tail as shown in D.) Bend the wire using your fingers and pliers.

[2] Hammer one or both sides of the connectors (**photo a**).
[3] Cut a length of 18-gauge wire ¾ in. (19mm) longer than the bead. String each bead onto its wire and turn a plain loop on each end (Basics, p. 7 and **photo b**).
[4] Working with your centerpiece bead, design a path for the wire.

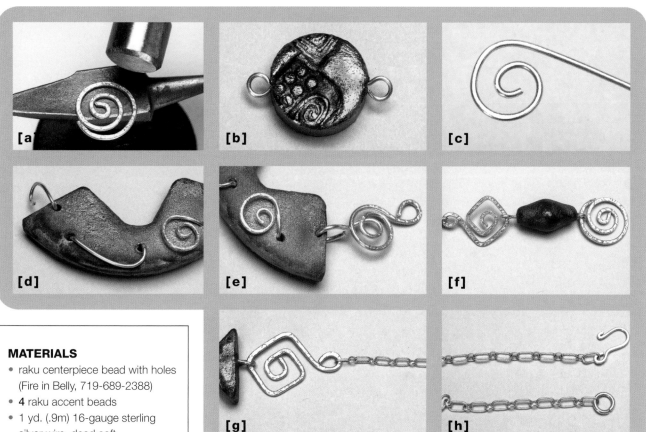

[a] [b] [c]

[d] [e] [f]

[g] [h]

MATERIALS

- raku centerpiece bead with holes (Fire in Belly, 719-689-2388)
- **4** raku accent beads
- 1 yd. (.9m) 16-gauge sterling silver wire, dead soft
- 8 in. (.2m) 18-gauge sterling silver wire, dead soft
- 5 in. (.13m) chain
- 1½ in. (38mm) 20-gauge wire or lobster claw clasp and split ring
- 7mm jump ring

Tools: chainnose pliers, roundnose pliers, ball peen hammer, wire cutters, anvil or bench block

Cut a piece of 16-gauge wire slightly longer than you think you'll need. Mine begins with a coil at one end (**photo c**).

[5] Working from front to back, go through any hole except one at the bead's edge. Run the wire loosely across the back of the bead and come to the front through a neighboring hole. Continue sewing, and make your last pass through a hole at the edge. Use the tail to make a loop as shown in **photo d**.

[6] Working with connector D, curve the straight tail slightly and go through the available hole at the edge. Keep the hammered side of the connector facing front. Bend the wire gently around the raku centerpiece (**photo e**).

[7] Link connectors and beads to build the sides of the necklace (**photo f**).

[8] Cut the chain in half. Slide the end link onto the loop on the last connector (**photo g**). Repeat on the other end of the necklace.

[9] Use 20-gauge wire to make a clasp (**figure 2**), hammer it slightly, and attach it to one end link. (Or attach a lobster claw using a split ring.) To finish the other end of the necklace, open a jump ring (Basics) and attach it to the end link of chain. Close the ring (**photo h**).

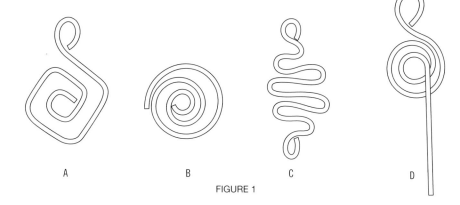

A   B   C   D

FIGURE 1

FIGURE 2

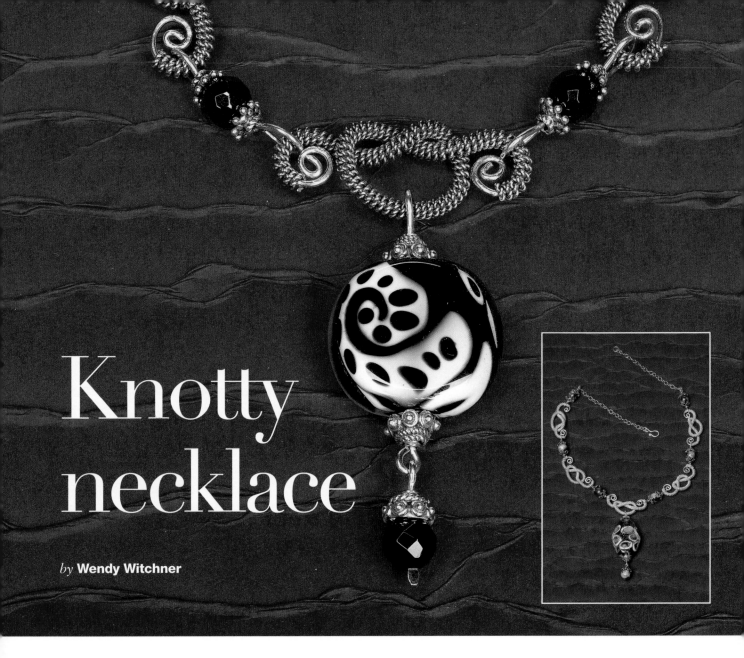

Knotty necklace

by **Wendy Witchner**

Twist wire coils into curls and knots for a fun look. Add a removable art glass pendant for a sophisticated look, or wear the choker without the pendant for a more casual style.

Necklace

[1] Cut a 24-in. (61cm) length of 24-gauge twisted wire and bend it in half.

[2] Cut a 5½-in. (14cm) length of 18-gauge wire and place it against the bend in the twisted wire. Hold the wires in position with your non-dominant hand, and with your dominant hand, wrap the twisted wire in a tight coil around the 18-gauge wire (**photo a**).

[3] When you reach the end of the first half of the twisted wire, turn the piece and wrap the other half.

[4] Slide the coil from the 18-gauge wire and trim it to 3½ in. (9cm). Slide the coil to the center of the 5½-in. length of 18-gauge wire and begin curving the wire into a circle until the wires cross (**photo b**).

[5] Tuck one end of the wire through the circle to form a knot shape (**photo c**). Refer to the template (**figure 1** or **2**) and adjust the knot's shape, keeping it centered.

[6] Use your fingers to curve one end of the wire up or down, depending on which template you are using (**photo d**). Repeat with the other side.

[7] Grasp the very tip of the 18-gauge wire with roundnose pliers and form a small, open loop toward the curve made in step 6 (**photo e**).

[8] Hold the loop in the jaws of flatnose pliers and roll the loop toward the knot in a flat open coil (**photo f**).

[9] Repeat steps 7–8 with the other side.

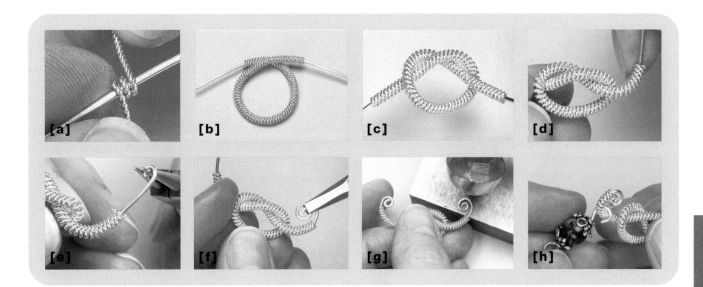

[a] [b] [c] [d]

[e] [f] [g] [h]

[10] Place the flat coil end of the wire knot on a block or anvil and use a hammer to flatten it (**photo g**). If your hammer is too big and you don't want to flatten the 24-gauge coil, use flatnose pliers to slightly open the flat coil before hammering. Repeat with the other side.

[11] Repeat steps 1–10 to make five wire knots.

[12] Cut a piece of 18-gauge wire 1 in. (2.5cm) longer than the 8mm bead. Make a loop (Basics, p. 7) at one end of the wire, large enough to attach to the coiled knot. String a bead cap, an 8mm bead, and a bead cap. Make a second loop in the same plane as the first. Repeat to make six 8mm bead units.

[13] Open a loop on a bead unit (Basics) and connect it to a knot component just below the flat coil (**photo h**). Close the loop.

[14] Continue connecting the bead links to the knot components. Start and end the necklace with a bead unit.

[15] Cut the chain in half so you have two pieces of equal length. Open the loop on an end bead link of the necklace and connect it to an end link of either piece of chain. Repeat at the other end of the necklace.

[16] Cut a 1¼-in. (3cm) piece of 18-gauge wire and follow the template (**figure 3**) to make a hook. Hammer the hook to harden it.

[17] Attach the loop on the clasp to either of the end links of chain.

[18] Attach a jump ring to the end link of the chain at the other end of the necklace.

Pendant

[1] String an 8mm bead and a bead cap on a head pin. Make a loop.

[2] Cut a piece of 18-gauge wire 2 in. (5cm) longer than the lampwork bead.

[3] Make a loop at one end of the wire and string a bead cap, the lampwork bead, and a bead cap. Make a second loop in the same plane as the first, large enough to attach to the center knot component on the necklace.

[4] Open the large loop and attach it to the bottom of the center knot component. Close the loop.

[5] Attach the bottom loop to the head-pin component from step 1 and close the loop.

MATERIALS

necklace 14–16 in. (36–41cm)

- lampwork bead (black and white bead by Glass Onion Studios, 877-444-5405, glassonion.biz; green and brown bead by Cindy Beads, 303-423-1616, cindybeads.com)
- **7** 8mm beads
- **13** bead caps to fit 8mm beads
- **2** bead caps for lampwork bead
- 10 ft. (3m) 24-gauge sterling silver twisted wire
- 4 ft (1.2m) 18-gauge sterling silver wire, dead-soft
- head pin
- 4–6 in. (10–15cm) large-link chain
- 6–8mm jump ring

Tools: chainnose pliers, flatnose pliers, roundnose pliers, ball peen hammer, anvil or steel block, wire cutters

FIGURE 1

FIGURE 2

FIGURE 3

Chips & chains

Create an elegant choker with inexpensive stone chips

by **Alice Korach**

Despite the glittering, expensive look of this crystal, pearl, and stone choker, it's extremely affordable; only the Swarovski crystals are costly, and you can substitute Czech fire-polished faceted beads for them with almost the same effect. A bonus is that the necklace looks difficult but is really easy if you can bend wire and count chain links. It will, however, take two or three evenings to string the 60–68 beaded bars through the chain strands.

Use four thin chains to space beads on head pins. Skipping one link more on the lower two chains than on the upper two makes a perfect curve. The back is a wide-link chain so it's adjustable. As you work, always go through the chains in the same order.

Starting the necklace

[1] Cut four chains: two 14½ in. (37cm) long and two 17½ in. (44.5cm). The beaded portion of the necklace will be 12¾ in. (32cm).

[2] To make the first beaded bar, cut a 1¼-in. (3cm) length of 24-gauge wire. Bend the end 1⁄16 in. (1.5mm) over into a tiny hook with chainnose pliers (**photo a**). Then press the hook closed with the pliers (**photo b**).

[3] String a 2mm pearl and go through the 6th link from one end of a 14½-in. chain. String a stone chip and the 5th link of the other 14½-in. chain. String a 6mm round crystal and go through the 5th link of a 17½-in. chain. String a chip and go

through the 6th link of the other 17½-in. chain (**photo c**). Note: If your chips are small, skip one less link on each chain.

[4] End the first beaded bar by stringing a 2mm pearl. Trim the remaining wire to ⅛ in. (3mm) (**photo d**) and fold the wire in half to create another hooked stopper as in step 2.

[5] For the next nine bars, skip two links on the 14½-in. chains (go through the third links from the

[a]

[b]

[c]

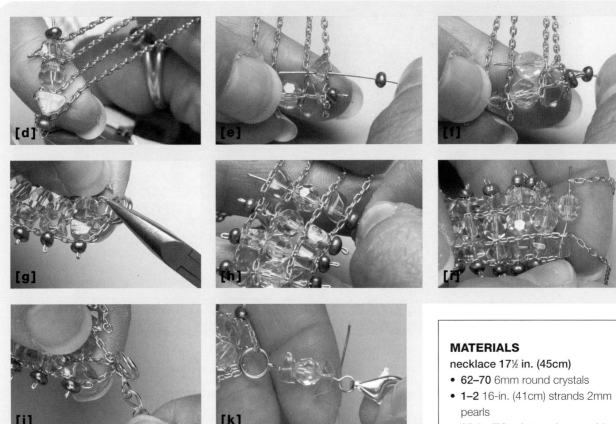

previous bar—**photo e**) and skip three links on the 17½-in. chains (go through the fourth links—**photo f**). Use larger chips between the 17½-in. chains because the space between them is a little wider than the space between the 14½-in. chains. Try to pick chips that are about the same thickness or use two thin chips in place of one thick one.

[6] Now that you have ten bars, use split-ring pliers to open one of the split rings and slip on the end links at the starting end of the necklace, bottom to top (**photo g**). Use chainnose pliers to turn the ring so that all the chains are fully on the split ring and the ring is closed.

Making the center section

[1] For the first bar of the center section, skip three links on all four chains (**photo h**).

[2] Make three bars spaced as step 5 above.

[3] Repeat steps 1–2 nine times for 40 center bars. For a longer necklace, repeat 11 times for 48 center bars.

[4] Make one more bar as in step 1.

Ending the necklace

[1] Make nine more bars spaced as in step 5 of "Starting the necklace." If your chain runs short, cut the needed additional length plus four or five links. Cut the short chain so the wire goes through the last link. Go through that link plus the end link of the extra piece (**photo i**). This join will not show.

[2] Cut off the excess chain, leaving six links on the top and bottom chains and five links on the middle chains.

[3] Open the other split ring with split-ring pliers and thread a 4-in. (10cm) length of open link chain onto it. The chain will hold the split ring open as you feed on the end links of the fine chain, bottom to top (**photo j**). Turn the split ring until all the chains are connected and the ring is closed.

[4] Cut a 2-in. (5cm) length of wire and begin a wrapped loop (Basics, p. 7). Pull the loop onto the split ring at the starting end of the necklace and complete the wrap. String a chip, a crystal, and a chip on the wire and begin a large wrapped loop. Pull the clasp into the loop (**photo k**). Complete the wraps.

[5] Cut another 2-in. (5cm) length of wire and begin a wrapped loop. Attach this to the end link of the back chain and complete the wrap. String a crystal, a chip, and a pearl. Then cut the excess wire, leaving ⅛ in. (3mm), and make a hooked stopper.

MATERIALS

necklace 17½ in. (45cm)

- **62–70** 6mm round crystals
- **1–2** 16-in. (41cm) strands 2mm pearls
- 30-in. (76cm) strand stone chips
- 7–8 ft. (2.1–2.4m) 24-gauge wire
- 54–76 in. (1.4–1.94m) 2.2mm cable chain
- 4 in. (10cm) large link chain
- lobster claw or hook clasp

Tools: chainnose pliers, roundnose pliers, split ring pliers, wire cutters, awl (optional)

CONTRIBUTORS

JoAnn Allard is a beader based in Massachusetts. Contact her at 67 Blacksmith Shop Rd., Box 682, W. Falmouth, MA 02574; (508) 548-4665; beadtree@aol.com.

Cheryl Assemi is the author of *Beaded Elegance* and *Beaded Elegance II*. She is also co-author of the Beaded Obsessions amulet book series with her family. You can order these books at beadgang.com.

Mindy Brooks is the editor of *Bead&Button* magazine. Contact her in care of the magazine.

Tina Czuba can be contacted at 110 S. Walkup Ave., Crystal Lake, IL 60014; (815) 356-1348.

Alethia Donathan owns DACS Beads, 1287 Kalani St. #102, Honolulu, HI 96817; (808) 842-7714; dacsbeads@aol.com.

Pat Duerfeldt can be contacted at 4412 Baltic St., Jacksonville, FL 32210; (904) 387-9717; pduerfel@fdn.com.

Wendy Ellsworth can be reached through ellsworthstudios.com.

Janet-Beth McCann Flynn can be contacted at (703) 759-2529 or janet@janetflynn.com.

Linda Gettings owns My Father's Beads at 702 W. State Street, Coopersburg, PA 18036.

LouAnn Hall can be contacted at (719) 495-9819 or lahall@divide.net.

Alice Korach, founding editor of *Bead&Button* magazine is now a glass artist. Her pâte de verre creations can be seen on her website, lostwaxglass.com.

Dina Krieg can be contacted at dinakrieg@hotmail.com.

Bindy Lambell can be contacted at (714) 895-4809 or bindy@bindy.com. You can see more of Bindy's work at bindy.com.

Marilyn K. Lowe can be contacted at 190 Park Ave., Merrick, NY 11566 or emkaylo@optonline.net.

Louise Malcolm is a beader and writer based in Wisconsin.

Irina Miech owns Eclectica, a bead store in Brookfield, WI and can be reached at 18900 W. Bluemound Rd., Brookfield, WI 53045-6082; (262) 641-0910; eclecticabeads.com.

Anna Nehs is an associate editor at *Bead&Button* magazine. Contact her in care of the magazine.

Lisa Norris can be contacted at hub12caps@erols.com.

Pam O'Connor is a contributing editor for *Bead&Button* magazine. Contact her at pampal@msn.com.

Linda Richmond can be contacted at 177 Hidden Harbor Lane, Sandpoint, ID 83864; (208) 265-7917; lindarichmond.com.

Karmen Schmidt teaches beading in Oregon and is president-elect of the Portland Bead Society. Contact her at Schmidt1@ccwebster.net.

Stacey Summerhill-Grady can be contacted at staceysummerhill@ earthlink.com.

Terri Torbeck can be contacted in care of *Bead&Button* magazine.

Lisa Olson Tune teaches beading in Oregon. Contact her at oralee5olson@comcast.net.

Paula Marie Walter can be contacted at 439 Arleta Ave., San Jose, CA 95128; (408) 275-1405; pwalter@earthlink.net.

Wendy Witchner is a contributing editor for *Bead&Button* and *BeadStyle* magazines. Contact her in care of the magazines.

Of course, contributor information is subject to change.

Contact *Bead&Button* and *BeadStyle* magazines at PO Box 1612, Waukesha, WI 53187-1612; (262) 796-8776. Visit our websites beadandbutton.com and beadstylemag.com to learn more about us.

INDEX